CHRONICALLY HAPPY

Joyful Living in Spite of Chronic Illness

CHRONICALLY HAPPY
Joyful Living in Spite of Chronic Illness

LORI HARTWELL

POETIC MEDIA PRESS
San Francisco

The epigraph on page xiv is from "Real Taste of Life: A Journal" © 2002 by Ken Ross. Reproduced by kind permission of Elisabeth Kübler-Ross, Ken Ross, and the Barbara Hogeson Agency, Inc.

"The Dash," on page 172, is reprinted by kind permission of Linda Ellis. © 1996 by Linda Ellis.

"Healing," on page 209, is from *The Body's Burning Fields: Poems of Illness and Healing.* © 1997 by Marguerite Bouvard. Reprinted by kind permission of Wind Publications, Nicholasville, Kentucky.

The material in this book is based on the author's experiences and opinions. This book should be used for informational purposes only, and all medical treatments, prescriptions, and strategies should be discussed by a patient with his or her own treating physician. Any advice that is inconsistent with a physician's advice should be disregarded.

ISBN 0-9722783-0-3

© 2002 Lori Hartwell
Poetic Media Press is a division of Poetic Media, Inc.
505 Beach Street, Penthouse, San Francisco, California 94133
http://www.poeticmedia.com

Printed in the United States of America

To the physicians, nurses, dietitians, social workers, patient-care technicians, research scientists, and all the other behind-the-scenes professionals who have a hand in caring for the chronically ill.

I would like to note, in particular, the doctors who have helped me over the years: Peter Breton, Gabriel Danovitch, Nicholas Di Domenico, Joseph Duflot, Robert Ettenger, Richard Fine, George Fischmann, Jeffrey Glick, Carl Grushkin, Josephine Hall, Stanley Jordan, Alan Koffler, Ellin Lieberman, Mohammad Malek, Alfred Pennisi, Thomas Rosenthal, Isidro Salusky, Christel Uittenbogaart, and Alan Wilkinson.

Your commitment, knowledge, bedside manner, and steadfast support helped me make the long climb from death's doorstep to a Chronically Happy life.

CONTENTS

FOREWORD

I met Lori Hartwell in the fall of 2001. We were brought
together by a common interest in helping chronically ill
people improve their day-to-day quality of life. The
occasion was a lunch, scheduled so I could pick Lori's
brain about an article I wanted to write on the "Miracle
of Dialysis" for iKidney.com (www.ikidney.com), an on-
line community for people with kidney disease. The
idea was to gently remind kidney disease patients that
dialysis gives the gift of life every day, despite its hard-
ships. I was struck with the concept after watching a
television feature on Jean Harlow, who died at twenty-
six in 1937. Harlow was arguably the Madonna of her
time, and she was lost to her fans merely because she
was born thirty years too soon. If Harlow's kidneys had
failed in the 1960s, she would be in the category of the
three hundred thousand individuals who undergo
dialysis several times every week of the year, and
who can live.

The article still has not been written. Lori Hartwell
spent the entire lunch telling me about a concept much
bigger than a feature about celebrity dialysis patients—
something Lori called "Chronically Happy." Chronically
Happy is how Lori has coped with thirty-five surgeries,
repeated kidney failure that punctuated a series of
unsuccessful transplants (until her last one, which is
working), a childhood stolen by illness, daily pain, medication, and lost childbearing ability. Chronically Happy
is how Lori Hartwell could sit across from me at lunch,
beaming with enthusiasm for life and burdened only by
the fact that she is too small, physically and financially, to handle all of the projects she wants to do.

Lori told me she was writing a book about Chronically
Happy, to share her life strategies. She told me her

advice addressed the most undertreated aspects of chronic illness: depression, anxiety, and low morale and self-esteem. Her guerrilla tactics, she argued, could help millions of chronically ill people manage such daily challenges as living with pain, working while ill, undergoing medical tests, and coping with financial difficulties.

Lori asked if I would take a draft home to read. It forever changed the way I would think about chronic illness. Here in Lori's little notebook was not a rant, a rage, or a howl by someone who certainly deserved to complain about what life dealt her. It was a veritable guidebook to finding happiness despite chronic illness, written by someone who has been and will be there for the rest of her days.

Poetic Media offered to help Lori publish the first edition of *Chronically Happy* and brought the extraordinary talents of editor Maggie Benson into the mix. The amazing result speaks for itself in the pages you're about to read.

Chronically Happy is an indispensable book for people who are chronically ill. It recognizes that the toughest issues of all in chronic illness are the day-to-day living issues. Whether you have kidney disease, HIV-AIDS, cancer, arthritis, diabetes, chronic hepatitis, asthma, or any other chronic illness or disability, *Chronically Happy* will bring more joy, productivity, love, enthusiasm, and optimism into your life.

Poetic Media is honored and privileged to introduce *Chronically Happy* to the world.

Jeffrey Makoff
President and Chief Executive Officer
Poetic Media, Inc.

ACKNOWLEDGMENTS

My heartfelt gratitude and appreciation go to all the people who helped make this book possible. I'd especially like to thank my family and friends for their encouragement throughout the project's development. A special thanks goes to Poetic Media and its president, Jeff Makoff, who immediately understood the *Chronically Happy* vision over our first lunch. His commitment, insight, and boldness in working with a new author helped make this book the best it could be.

I'd like to express my appreciation to the team that worked on *Chronically Happy*: Maggie Benson, whose editorial talent and dedication helped take the book to the next level; Cecily Barnes for the many hours she devoted to careful research, investigation, and verification; Tracy Buck, the cartoonist, your skill blows me away; and David Meirik for the creative layout and cover design. I am also grateful to the Patient Advocate Foundation's Sheldon Weinhaus for sharing his expertise on health insurance, the Americans with Disabilities Act, and the Family Medical Leave Act.

I am deeply appreciative of the many people who willingly shared their stories with me. Your candor made this book what it is.

Last, but not least, I would like to thank my mom, Marlene, and my husband, Dean, for their love, encouragement, and unwavering support.

CHRONICALLY HAPPY

Joyful Living in Spite of Chronic Illness

People are like stained-glass windows.
They sparkle and shine when the sun is out,
but when the darkness sets in, their true beauty
is revealed only if there is a light from within.

—Elisabeth Kübler-Ross

INTRODUCTION

An estimated one hundred million Americans have a chronic illness.

I was stunned to read this statistic, which I stumbled across in the *New England Journal of Medicine* in 1999. Though I had no idea so many people, like me, were living with chronic conditions, I had long been convinced that our numbers were growing. At the same time, I'd noticed that the resources available to us weren't meeting a vital need. Quite a bit had been written about getting through an illness, but, I realized, few works had been dedicated to living a joyful, full life in spite of disease.

For more than three decades, I have lived through dialysis, dozens of surgeries, unsuccessful transplants, and the constant pokes and prods of every medical instrument known to humankind.

My kidneys began to deteriorate when I was two years old. By the time I turned twelve, they shut down completely and were removed. I was left to depend on a dialysis machine to remove liquid waste and extra fluids from my body.

During the next several years, I was fortunate enough to receive a donor kidney not once, but twice—and unfortunate enough to reject both. The final blow came when my doctors told me my chances were "slim to none" that I would undergo a successful transplant.

I was in my young twenties when I heard this news, and I felt as if my life had been pulled out from under me. All the years I'd spent living with a chronic disease had finally caught up with me. I came to realize that I would likely have to spend the rest of my days chained to dialysis. I felt isolated, alone, and angry as hell. I didn't know it at the time, but it was that anger that ignited my emotional healing. It led me to the realization that I had two choices: sink further into bitterness and despair or beat the odds and live the fullest life I could with the time I had left. I thought hard, weighed the options—and chose life.

I started discovering little tricks that made living easier; principles I will share with you throughout this book. My goal was quality of life, and to achieve it I knew I had to take care of the whole me. The strategies I devised honored both my body and my spirit and have enabled me, each day, to continue making the choice of life.

One day in 1990, as I camped with my friends in the fresh air of Southern California's mountains, I received life-changing news. My transplant coordinator found a donor and told me to get to the hospital right away. Though haunted by past disappointments and discouraging medical statistics, I decided to go for it. Nearing the age of twenty-four, I didn't want to live the rest of my life dependent on a machine if I didn't have to.

That transplant turned out to be a perfect match. My new kidney continues to work beautifully and has allowed me a freedom that I appreciate each day. I will be forever grateful to my organ donor and his family's brave and selfless decision to give me the gift of life.

Although an unspeakable blessing, transplantation is not a cure. It is just one form of treatment for kidney failure. I must take medication every day and have been diagnosed with some of the additional illnesses—such as arthritis—that kidney disease can cause. I also live with the knowledge that at any time my body could reject the kidney, and I would have to return to dialysis.

There are millions of other Americans riding the same physical and emotional roller coaster of chronic illness. We all share common threads of emotion: anger, guilt, fear of the unknown, depression, and the mind-boggling question, "Why me?" I wrote *Chronically*

Happy to help people face these feelings and abandon the crippling mental barriers that go hand-in-hand with chronic disease.

The stories, suggestions, and principles set forth on these pages reflect the twists and turns I've traveled along my journey. My greatest hope is that you will join me in searching for the precious nuggets—those simple steps you can take that will help you realize your dreams.

1

DIAGNOSIS

You watch as your doctor's mouth moves, but the words coming out just don't make sense. You feign understanding with an occasional nod, but inside you are tumbling head to heel, trying to unravel the sentence he spoke when you first sat down. "Me? I have a chronic illness?" Over the next few weeks, the shock will wear off, but a range of other difficult emotions awaits you. I'm here to tell you can and will get beyond these feelings and live a fulfilling life. Your life is not over; it's just begun.

What lies behind us and what lies ahead of us are tiny matters compared to what lives within us.

—Oliver Wendell Holmes

DON'T REMEMBER the first time someone said to me, "You have a chronic illness." I was a toddler at the onset of my disease, but through the years, my family has repeatedly told the story of the winter day my mother rushed me to the hospital, my temperature surging and stomach bloated. It is the retelling of this story that has created my memory.

The year was 1968, and I was two years old. I hadn't eaten in two days, and despite submerging me in cold baths, my mother hadn't been able to bring my fever down. She took me to Sunrise Hospital in Las Vegas, where the medical staff was so baffled by my symptoms they didn't know how to treat me. I was growing sicker by the moment, so they promptly sent me to Children's Hospital in Los Angeles, which was better equipped to deal with serious ailments in children.

After a battery of tests at Children's, the specialists pinpointed the problem: complete kidney failure. At the time, the cause was a mystery, but, in later years, they diagnosed me with hemolytic uremic syndrome, a disease brought on by *E.coli* bacteria.

The medical team hooked my twenty-two-pound frame up to a dialysis machine, which, to me, looked like a modified washing machine. The contraption pulled my blood out, cleaned it, and then pumped it back in. The treatment kept me going for several weeks—until the day the tubing burst, and I nearly bled to death.

Ironically, this mishap ended up saving my life. As the blood drained out of me, so did the *E.coli* bacteria, relieving the stress on my kidneys, and enabling them to work again.

My diseased kidneys fought off dialysis for ten years, but wreaked havoc in other ways on my body. Mainly, they caused my blood pressure to rise uncontrollably, which made brain damage and stroke continuous threats.

Medications and a restricted diet controlled my blood pressure until I was twelve years old, living in Florida with my mom. It was here the medications and diet stopped working. Since I didn't have access to the specialists I needed, my mom took me back to Children's. With no money, my mom and my cherished black poodle, Pepi, and I packed up our gold-colored Oldsmobile and started the trek across the country. I was on my way to hear one of the most difficult diagnoses I would ever receive.

Propped up in the front seat of the Olds, I was going downhill fast. I couldn't lie down and breathe at the same time. My mom would drive all day and I would sleep with my head on the window. At night I would sit up in the hotel room and watch television. I learned later I had been in congestive heart failure.

When we arrived in Los Angeles, we drove immediately to the hospital. My kidneys were failing again, and I had to go on dialysis right away. I underwent an emergency operation so the medical team could access my veins for dialysis. Sometime later, they removed my kidneys altogether.

During the following twelve years, I lived through dialysis treatments, three transplants, and two rejections. Each transplant brought renewed hope; each rejection would send me reeling. It took me years to learn how to manage the feelings that came along with the constant diagnoses, the seemingly endless stream of bad news.

Even after my successful transplant in 1990 when I was twenty-four years old, the diagnoses didn't stop. Since then, I've been treated for arthritis, osteoporosis, renal failure, and, I learned recently, I will likely have to have a hysterectomy. After years of taking immunosuppressant medications, I'm at a high risk for uterine cancer, and having a hysterectomy is the best way to rid my body of the precancerous cells.

In short, I have felt the way you may be feeling, swinging from anger to sadness, from "I'm going to beat this!" to "Why me?" I've been crushed in the vice grip, battling with depression, grief, and hope-shattering medical statistics and prognoses. I'm here to tell you that you can and will get beyond these feelings.

The first step is to acknowledge and deal with them; understanding what these feelings are and anticipating when they will surface are key steps in rebuilding your hopes, your future, and your dreams.

FACING THE EMOTIONS OF A CHRONIC ILLNESS
No More 'Untimely Ouches'

During my many medical procedures, I've had to endure hundreds of needle pricks. When I was younger, I would never complain about the number of sticks the nurses made. Consequently, they repeatedly told me what a good patient I was. In reality, those needles hurt! I wanted to cry and scream at the person who kept poking me. Most often I was silent and tried to be as accommodating as possible.

What happened to the feelings boiling inside? I would vent them in other, nonrelated ways. I would cuss out drivers on the way home from the hospital, or I would snap at my mom.

Later, I learned that I had been disassociating my feelings. It was as though someone stepped on my foot, and I would yell, "Ouch!" two weeks later. My compliant attitude had been a survival tool, one that was hurting me. By not expressing my true feelings, I was telling myself that my physical or emotional instincts were incorrect and should not be trusted. I consequently had a hard time expressing how I really felt.

To deal with the problem, I learned that when an emotion came up, I had to consciously ask myself, "How do you feel, Lori?" and then I had to acknowledge it immediately. "No more untimely ouches!" became my motto.

This is my challenge to you. Address your hurts as they arise. If you have been recently diagnosed with a chronic illness or are dealing with one in a long list of diagnoses, it is critical that you identify your feelings so you can cope with them.

Research has shown most people go through similar emotional stages when they are met with severe loss, such as the death of a loved one or the diagnosis of a severe illness.[1] Through my many diagnoses, I've noticed that I first go through a shock phase, then I slip into denial. These feelings are followed by anger and fear, grief, and sometimes depression. Only after I've passed through the gamut am I able to reach the final stage—acceptance, where I find a way to live with the diagnosis, pick up and move on.

This book will talk mostly about picking up and moving on, but before we get into strategies for living with chronic illness, we have to sort through the difficult emotions that can be brought on by the diagnosis itself.

Life appears to me too short to be spent in nursing animosity or registering wrongs.

—Charlotte Brontë

Shock: This Can't Be Happening

Some of you may have struggled with unexplained symptoms before learning what ails you. This often happens to people who have less-understood diseases for which there is no test, such as chronic fatigue syndrome. For you, a diagnosis can be a welcome relief. It carries the promise of treatment and potential recovery.

Others, however, such as those with HIV or cancer, may have few noticeable symptoms before being diagnosed. In these cases, the news can result in life-halting shock.

Lance Armstrong, champion cyclist and winner of the Tour de France, recalls his feelings after learning he had testicular cancer in his biography *It's Not About the Bike: My Journey Back to Life.* After an initial consultation, the doctor who diagnosed Armstrong scheduled surgery for the next day. Here's what happened when Armstrong left that appointment:

> For the first time in my life, I drove slowly. I was in shock. I drifted through the streets in first gear, without even the energy to press the gas pedal. As I puttered along, I questioned everything: my world, my profession, myself. I had left the house an indestructible twenty-five-year-old, bulletproof. Cancer would change everything for me,

I realized; it wouldn't just derail my career, it would deprive me of my entire definition of who I was.[2]

Denial: This Isn't Happening to Me

Many people find it difficult to accept they have an illness, before and after diagnosis. In Armstrong's case, denial prevented him from acting on his symptoms.

[Cycling] is a sport of self-abuse. Everything hurts. Your back hurts, your feet hurt, your hands hurt, your neck hurts, your legs hurt, and of course, your butt hurts. So no, I didn't pay attention to the fact that I didn't feel well in 1996. When my right testicle became slightly swollen that winter, I told myself to live with it because I figured it was something I had done to myself on my bike.[3]

Some level of denial, like Armstrong's, is natural. Why would Armstrong, a world-class athlete, believe he was sick? Some denial after we hear the diagnosis is also understandable. It can be protective, acting as a buffer between ourselves and a harsh truth we are not yet prepared to face.

If the denial goes on, however, it can be harmful. The longer you refuse to face the truth, the longer it will take to work around the losses and map out a new future. If denial delays necessary treatment, it can be disastrous. Denial will not make the illness disappear or the raw feelings go away.

Matthew Dubiner, a retired teacher who taught science for thirty-five years, was diagnosed with a form of dementia after several seizures. He describes his feelings after hearing the news of his illness:

Have I been given a diagnosis? Yes! Do I dispute my doctor's diagnosis? Yes! When I was told, I was filled with a fierce anger and an agitation that could not be calmed. Why me? This is not fair! This left me emotionally splintered. My reaction, in the face of all the evidence, was total denial. By employing an elaborate set of rationales, I was able to deflect reality. Despite my protestation that I was as capable as ever, those around me, especially my wife, saw more than I did, or maybe, more apropos, saw less of me.

Denial isn't always so obvious. A chronic illness is just that—chronic. The "chronicity" of the disease is a breeding ground for denial because of the way it slowly changes your life and behavior patterns. An example is my arthritis. Renal disease causes bone loss, which contributes to arthritis. It has been part of my life much longer than I dared to recognize.

When the symptoms first started, I made excuses for no longer playing sports. "I'm too busy," or "I'm too tired," I'd tell my friends, rather than admit quick movements were just too painful. I agonized over the cold weather arriving because, "I don't like the cold," not because my joints ached. I gave up my high-heel shoes for flats because, "Flats are more practical," not because the heels shot spikes through my legs with each step.

I did not want to believe I had another problem related to my kidney disease. Had I addressed the arthritis head on, I may have ended up in better shape today. For one, I know now I could have continued to exercise (under the supervision of a trained specialist) despite the pain. By slowing down, I may actually have made the problem worse.[4]

As you can see from my situation, the first step to living with an illness is to acknowledge you have one. By denying you are ill, you could be giving up valuable time for medical treatment, as well as physical, psychological, and spiritual adjustment. Don't take the gamble!

Anger: Yes, You Got a Raw Deal!

Anger is an inevitable part of the unsavory package when you're diagnosed with a chronic illness. There's no way around it. You got a raw deal! You have sustained a devastating loss of health, which must be acknowledged, felt, and grieved. The tricky thing about anger is it will not go away if you ignore it. Anger, left unaddressed, can negatively affect you and your relationships. My friend Maria Hsieh recalls how she discovered she was deeply angry over her diagnosis with renal failure:

> I was shopping at JCPenney. A clerk almost ran into me while I was walking down an aisle looking for a pair of sunglasses. I did not even realize how angry I was. Even though I knew it was an accident, she was in the wrong place at the wrong time and became the prime target for my anger. I just lost it, saying, 'You better watch it,' with a look that would kill, something totally out of my character. She quickly moved and got out of my way. After this incident I realized how the anger was bottling up inside of me. Inappropriate comments were a way of releasing the anger. My anger was projecting on other people and pushing them away. This was the first time my anger surfaced noticeably, and I could see if I didn't address the feeling, it would certainly take over my life and alienate my friends and family.

We all have something to be really angry about it. It's appropriate to let out those feelings, but it's equally important to be mindful of how you do it.

If your anger persists, I suggest you be clear with your friends and family: "I'm not mad at you; I'm mad at the world. This all feels so unfair." By showing your loved ones your vulnerability, rather than growling at them, you'll create a safe place to talk about your feelings. Such an approach is more likely to lead to the kind

of reception you need: one of listening and understanding, not frustration.

Pinpoint the Cause of Your Anger

It is also helpful to get to the root of the anger, then
work it out. I was furious when my physician recently
broke the news that I would likely need a hysterectomy!
When I looked closely at the situation I realized, yes,
I'm angry that I may never give birth to a child. What
got me really upset, however, is that I've lost the freedom to make the choice. By homing in on the reason for
my anger, I began to conquer it: I may have to give up
the choice to have a child, but I am not giving up the
choice to live a happy life.

I focused on reaffirming my life by setting my body
in motion. I went for a walk. I took a trip to the local ice
rink and watched the kids slide and fall. I soaked in the
sensation of the cool air and upbeat music. It reminded
me to enjoy what I have right now—and let go of the
things I can't have. I got informed. I spoke at length
with my gynecologist, Dr. Josephine Hall. She told me I
have more choices than I think. For one, she said, I can

PEN AND PAPER: *Write a List of What You CAN Do*

Throughout this book, you'll find several references to what I call Lori's Toolbox. This is a metaphorical kit filled with useful devices to help you push past barriers or slog through unshakable funks. The first, and possibly the most indispensable, instruments in your box are pen and paper. I'm a big believer in writing things down, and you'll find several exercises where I encourage you to jot your thoughts on paper. Doing this has a magical way of making ideas realities, keeping us focused on goals, and making us realize how far we've come.

With a chronic illness, it's so easy to concentrate on the negatives. With the following exercise, I'd like you to recognize the things you CAN do, despite your loss.

find a surrogate mother. This gave me hope. I don't know if I'll take this route, but it is uplifting to know I have options.

There are many books on anger and how to get through the hard times, including *The Anger Workbook*.[5] If we carry anger inside of us, it can slowly eat our souls away. Or, as Ralph Waldo Emerson put it, "For every minute you remain angry, you give up sixty seconds of peace of mind."

Fear: Don't Get Paralyzed by the What-Ifs

Fear is a powerful emotion, one that can leave us doe-in-the-headlights panicked. When Franklin Roosevelt said to Depression-weary Americans in his 1933 inaugural speech, "The only thing we have to fear is fear itself," he was talking about this kind of paralysis. He was urging Americans to get on with their lives, to

Here are some ideas to help you get started.

Can You Read?—Perhaps you could learn a new language, join a book club, or increase your formal education through correspondence courses.

Can You Write?—Compose a poem, send a note to someone in need of a good word, or make a new friend via e-mail.

Can You Work with Your Hands?—How about woodworking, painting, or sculpting?

If all you have energy for today is talking on the phone, write that down and count it as a victory—and in the meantime, take the opportunity to bless someone's life with encouragement, support, and a listening ear. As you are reminded of more things you can do, add them to the list, and take daily encouragement that you now have written proof that life is far from over.

muster up a little "irrational exuberance" so the economy would get moving again. I think his famous words would have been more accurate if they read: "The only thing we have to fear is fear itself—and an unskilled IV nurse."

When you are diagnosed with a chronic illness, it's easy to become mentally stuck by the terrifying what-ifs. "What if I can't work?", "What if I end up in the hospital?", "What if I lose the ability to walk?"

It helps to get educated about your illness and to create a game plan should your worst-case scenario become a reality.

By visualizing the worst thing that could happen and seeing yourself continuing to create value in your life, you take the power away from the fear. I used this strategy with my knees. I kept thinking, "What if my knees go? I just won't want to live!" The more I fretted, the

more trouble they gave me. The mental gymnastics were out of control, and I decided it would be healthier to take action, rather than sit around and worry.

I did everything I could to keep my knees in the best possible shape. I determined that if, despite these efforts, my knees were still going to give out, then "Damn the torpedoes!" I would just do more with my mind and my hands. Guess what happened after I stopped dwelling on my knees? They felt better! No, my knees are not perfect, and they still give me pain. I just don't give them the power to wreck my day or my plans for the future.

Franklin's wife, Eleanor Roosevelt, said this about fear: "You gain strength, courage, and confidence by every experience in which you really stop to look fear in the face. You are able to say to yourself, 'I have lived through this horror. I can take the next thing that comes along.' You must do the thing you think you cannot do."

Grief: It's Okay to Be Sad

Believe it or not, I started to learn to grieve in my early twenties when a teacher in a singing class asked me to

IT ISN'T YOU, IT'S THE MEDS

As you sort through your postdiagnosis feelings, be aware of how your medications may be affecting you. Many people with chronic illness take a laundry list of drugs that can intensify feelings of anger, frustration, agitation, and depression.

I know firsthand what a common anti-inflammatory steroid can do to your mind. While taking it, I felt as if I were on an emotional roller coaster with no way to get off.

One day I would be sky-high and the next day I felt as if the world were coming to an end. I would cry over the silliest of things, knowing they were silly, but I couldn't stop myself. Daily tasks seemed overly complicated, and the simplest of chores agitated me.

The only thing that gave me comfort was confiding in a fellow patient. She said to me, "Lori, don't worry. It isn't you, it's the meds."

Read the side effects of medications before taking them. If you feel the treatment is causing a problem, you should speak to your doctor about finding a solution.

sing loud enough for her to hear. Despite her persistence, all I could manage was a whisper. Finally, she said, "Lori, you're not used to being heard, are you?" Her words released a wellspring of sadness in me, and I broke down and cried in front of the class.

I couldn't stop. I cried so hard I could barely breathe; something I had never experienced before. For the first time, I acknowledged that life had treated me unfairly and that it hurt, terribly. The painful episode marked a turning point. I learned I had to let out my sadness— or else it would overtake me.

Grieving is one of the most important steps in accepting your losses and moving on. The feelings build up and they have to be released, like a valve in a dam.

Throw Yourself a Pity Party

On a recent night, as I tried to go to sleep, all I could think about was how angry I was. My body ached, and I was tired. Why do I have to have a hysterectomy? Why do my knees ache? I exercise, I watch what I eat, but still the pain is there. What choices do I have?

I felt out of control, my blood was boiling inside. The physical and emotional pain of my chronic illness— and yet another distressing diagnosis—were slowly creeping in and robbing me of basic enjoyments in life.

My husband asked me, "Are you all right?" Tears were rolling down my cheeks.

"I worry about walking long distances," I told him. "Will my knees give out? I can't play tag with my niece and nephew anymore. It hurts to sit on the floor with them. And now I can't even make the choice of whether we will have children. I feel so inadequate. Right now all I can focus on is what I do not have."

This is called a Pity Party, and I needed it, badly. Pity Parties are okay if they do not last very long and you invite loved ones, like my caring husband Dean.

By the end of our conversation I had a trash can full of Kleenex. Once again my anger turned into sadness, then slowly into acceptance. I allowed myself to grieve my losses, again. No matter how many negative diagnoses I hear, I know I'll have to grieve each one.

The world is full of suffering, it is true, but full, also, of the overcoming of it.

—Helen Keller

Depression: If You Need Help, Get It

While grief can help us move on from difficult losses, depression can keep us stuck there. Mandy Gordon became depressed after acknowledging her chronic fatigue syndrome was not going to go away. For years she had sought second opinions and went from doctor's office to doctor's office in search of someone who would "cure her." When she finally accepted she would not get better, the despair set in. "I got very depressed. I spent lots of time in tears. I was grieving for the person I was. Things used to be very easy," she recalls. "Things that I would fit into a day's work, like shopping or getting my hair cut, are now very hard. I felt very sad and hopeless."

Gordon worked through her depression, though she still occasionally struggles. Today, she is in the process of configuring her old life to the one that once was. "I just have to plan my days very carefully. I have to make sure I give myself a little target, something to accomplish each day. And however awful it seems having to get out of bed in the morning, I do. I know from past experience that if you do get up, get dressed, and get washed, the day looks a little bit brighter."

Symptoms of Depression

Research has shown that people with chronic illness have higher rates of depression. Some sources estimate the condition is twice as prevalent with the chronically ill as with the physically healthy,[6] and Lee Shirey, author of "Depression: A Treatable Disease," estimates 25 to 33 percent of people with chronic disease also suffer depression.[7]

The prevalence of depression is not a reason for you or your doctors to treat depression as "normal" and leave it unaddressed. In an article on depression and people with chronic conditions, depression specialist Dr. Arthur Rifkin writes:

> I believe that the most common misconception preventing correct diagnosis [of depression among the chronically ill] is that depression in such a situation is understandable and does not represent a treatable mental disorder. This notion

is shared by patients and physicians alike. Disentangling normal feelings from symptoms of a mental disorder requires careful attention to details of symptoms, their longitudinal development, and historical details ... [Depression] should not be dismissed because it is 'understandable' in particular situations, but rather, it should be differentiated from overlapping symptoms of the physical disorder and treated.[8]

So how can you tell if you are reasonably blue because of this life-shaking news or if you are mired in a full-blown clinical depression? Talk to your doctor; he is trained to recognize the signs. There are many options these days for people with depression, and your doctor will be able to refer you to the proper resources.

In the meantime, be on the lookout for these symptoms, several of which would occur every day over an extended period of time:

- A depressed mood
- A marked diminished interest or pleasure in taking part in any activities
- Insomnia or hypersomnia
- Psycho-motor agitation or retardation
- Fatigue or loss of energy
- Feelings of worthlessness or excessive or inappropriate guilt
- Diminished ability to think or concentrate or indecisiveness
- Significant weight loss or weight gain when not dieting
- Recurrent thoughts of death or suicide[9]

Since some of these symptoms, such as fatigue and weight fluctuations, may be caused by the illness itself, depression can be difficult to discern.[10]

Another tricky point is that depression may advance as your condition does. "Depression is one of the most common—and potentially dangerous—complications of every chronic condition because it often worsens with the condition," Shirey writes.[11] The key is to be aware; check in with yourself and, most importantly, get help if you need it.

Seeking Aid for Depression

Loved ones, support networks, professional counselors, and, for some, medication are ways to get through the depression. After his diagnosis with dementia, Matthew Dubiner knew his depression was harming him and his relationships. He turned to his family and an Alzheimer's support network for help.

> Each of us rides the waves of happiness and depression, and I had plummeted to the depths at the trough of despair. I was losing me! At the same time, my anger and denial were drowning everyone who cared about me. These negatives carried over into every aspect of my family's daily lives. ... This was two years ago. Today, though a great deal of anger remains lodged within me, I am filled with a tremendous sense of gratitude for my wife, my children, and for the Long Island Alzheimer's Foundation. These horrific feelings have undergone a small yet meaningful metamorphosis. By being involved and active in understanding my situation, I have begun to channel my energies in a manner that is positive rather than one which saw only destruction as its end product.

Like Dubiner, when I was close to bottoming out, I found much-needed support through an organized group. In my case, it was Al-Anon, a support program designed for friends and loved ones of alcoholics. This lively and compassionate organization not only helped me understand my family dynamics, it also

Destiny is not a matter of chance, it is a matter of choice; it is not a thing to be waited for, it is a thing to be achieved.

—William Jennings Bryan

21

helped me navigate my journey with a chronic illness. Everyone's solution will be unique. Find the one that works for you.

Acceptance: The Key to Getting on with Living

Acceptance of a chronic illness takes time. It is important to identify and experience the different emotional stages that come along with diagnoses before reaching acceptance. There are no short cuts.

Also helpful is realizing there is no shame in having a chronic illness—that it isn't anyone's fault. I've come to understand that life isn't fair, and if I try to keep score and compare myself to others, I will surely lose.

The bottom line is we can accept that we have a chronic illness and make the best life we possibly can, or we can shrivel up with our anger. I choose life.

WHAT'S NEXT?
Okay, I'm Ready to Move Forward—But How?

Still, even after you've faced the feelings surrounding your diagnosis, and you are ready to "choose life," it is often hard to know where to begin. How do you care for your children, go to work, sustain your relationships—all the things you used to do? Such matters, things you may have "turned off" as you coped with the initial emotions of diagnosis, can suddenly press in at you from all angles.

My advice: Tackle one issue at a time. Foremost is your *health*. Get informed about your illness. Take control of your medical care. Listen to your feelings, listen to your body. When you tune in to yourself, you build up a backlog of strength that you'll be able to tap when you are ready to tackle the rest of life's issues.

Adjusting to chronic illness takes time, but you will soon begin to see how to regain a full life. In the following pages, I will describe how I have navigated my way through the hills and valleys of illness. With this guide—and plenty of effort, awareness, and spirit—I'm confident you will make your way, too.

2

BE INFORMED, GET ADJUSTED

Education has the power to ease the transition in the months after your diagnosis, but obtaining the facts you need isn't always easy. In this chapter you'll find out how to inform yourself by working with your healthcare providers, through your own research, and through support groups. Armed with knowledge, you'll be able to take control of your health and your future.

The beginning of wisdom is to call things by their right names.

—Chinese Proverb

I AM AMAZED at how often people with chronic illness get a diagnosis and little else. On countless occasions I've asked fellow patients simple questions about their conditions, only to discover they don't understand the basics. They haven't been given, or haven't sought out, the information.

In the first months after diagnosis, information is your most powerful ally. The more you educate yourself, the more likely you'll choose the right doctor, make good decisions about your healthcare, gain confidence, and feel less out of control. Of course, getting the information you need isn't always easy. First, you'll have to learn the language of your illness. This entails understanding the hailstorm of technical medical terms, medications, and treatments headed your way.

WORKING INSIDE THE SYSTEM

Team with Your Doctors

Becoming educated about your illness is something you must want to do. No one will force the information on you. Instead, your doctor might simply rattle on, using terms you don't understand. If you don't tell her to slow down and ask her some questions, you will miss the opportunity to become actively involved in your own care. Many times I have positively influenced the course of my treatment because I did my homework and found the right issues to probe.

Translating 'Medicalese'

The first step in information gathering is unraveling your physician's "medicalese." Medical jargon is difficult for the uninitiated to sort through, so don't feel bad if it takes you a while to catch on. As proof, here's a humorous anecdote that's made rounds through the medical community: A patient checked into the emergency room, complaining of difficulty breathing. The doctor examined him and wrote down a few notes on the patient's chart. When the doctor left the room, the patient reviewed the notes. He became flushed with anger. When the doctor returned, he snapped, "Why'd you describe me as a son of a bitch?" The physician patiently explained, "SOB is shorthand for 'shortness of breath."

Physicians use hundreds of acronyms to describe symptoms, tests, medications, and treatments. These acronyms—coupled with the fact that doctors are justifiably stereotyped for bad penmanship—are a breeding ground for confusion. Never take the quick notes in your chart personally, and always ask if you don't understand something a medical provider has written or said. Once you've learned the basics of your illness and the eight million new words that go along with it, you'll find it easier to navigate your care. Here are some ways to work through medicalese:

Ask Questions—By the end of this chapter, these words will ring in your ears like a mantra. Ask questions, ask questions, ask questions. Inquiring about things you don't understand is the best way to figure them out.

Take Notes at Doctor Visits—This is critical, especially in the rushed environment of the physician's office. Don't be afraid to ask your doctor for spellings of unfamiliar words. He will appreciate your desire to get informed and the resulting thoughtful questions.

Take Someone with You to the Visit—Especially right after your diagnosis, it can be difficult to concentrate on, let alone absorb, what your doctor is saying, so note-taking may be impossible. Take someone you love and trust, and ask that person to pay attention for you. Of course, it is also critical to have that person there to lend support and understanding. Later, you can sit down together and go through the notes at your own pace. This way you will be sure you didn't miss—or misinterpret—anything.

Research—In the more relaxed environment of your home or library, take out the notes from your visit and unearth as much information as you can. Use the terms as keywords for Internet searches. At the library, ask for help on finding the latest articles on your condition. If you feel too sick, ask your partner or a friend to copy off or print out some articles for you. In the beginning, expect to feel overwhelmed and confused, but stick with it. The language will grow familiar, and before long, you, too, will be fluent in medicalese.

Take Notes Again—Take notes while you are researching. Keep a special sheet reserved for questions that crop up as you siphon through the information. At your next doctor visit, pull out your questions and fire away.

The Doctor Said What?!

Following is even more evidence that you can't always take what the doctor writes in your chart personally. These physicians' comments were compiled from actual medical transcriptions and are featured in Richard Lederer's 1996 book, *Fractured English.*[1]

- She has no rigors or shaking chills, but her husband states that she was very hot in bed last night.
- He was eating his tray so I didn't examine him.
- The patient is a Catholic nun currently in between missionaries.
- For his impotence we will discontinue the meds and let his wife handle him.
- The patient was bitten by a bat as he walked down the street on his thumb.
- Patient's wife hit him over the head with an ironing board, which now has six stitches in it.
- This fifty-four-year-old female is complaining of abdominal cramps with BMs on the one hand and constipation on the other.
- Healthy-appearing, decrepit sixty-nine-year-old white female, mentally alert but forgetful.
- When she fainted, her eyes rolled around the room.
- He states he hit his head on his forehead.
- She is to refrain from sexual intercourse until I see her in the office.
- Patient stated that if she would lie down, within two or three minutes something would come across her abdomen and knock her up.
- Patient has chest pains if she lies on her left side for over a year.

28

Finding Dr. Right

As if it's not hard enough to muck through the difficult new terminology, you will likely be faced with another challenge during the postdiagnosis stage: finding a new doctor. The physician who made your initial diagnosis will often advise you to go to a specialist for continuing care, or you may be dissatisfied with your doctor's assessment and desire a second opinion. As a result, you'll probably meet with several practitioners in the coming months. Finding the right one is critical.

When you have a chronic illness, the relationship with your doctor is like a marriage. Together you will be tackling some of the most difficult decisions of your life. You must select your physician with almost the same care you pick your spouse. If your doctor is not "marriage material," keep on searching. Once you find "the one," chances are greater that you'll, ahem, live Chronically Happy ever after.

I've had my share of physicians. I spent most of my younger years at university hospitals, where it seemed I had a new doctor every month. Some were sensitive, creative professionals, while others were arrogant, "I'm-the-boss, my-time-is-too-valuable-to-answer-your-questions" types, who seemed to dictate care plans, rather than involve me in the process. I learned a lot from those experiences. Mainly, I discovered *I have the right to choose* who cares for me, rather than accept whoever happens to be on shift that day.

I also discovered what kind of doctor I like: one who understands the difficulties I am going through, listens to my side of the story and involves me in decisions. Good doctors focus on "what's right" with their patients. I could write a long list of what's wrong with me, and if I focused on that all the time, I'd never get out of bed in the morning. So I think a good doctor is, in a sense, a

A PRESCRIPTION FOR DR. RIGHT: *Write Your Own*

 A girl has a right to dream, right? Remember when you were younger, and you and your friends would write down the qualities of the "Dream Guy?" 1. Tall 2. Funny 3. Cool Dresser 4. Romantic ... You get the picture. Well, times have changed. Now, it's more important to find the perfect doctor than the Perfect Ten. It may seem strange to revert to junior-high tactics to find a physician, but writing down Dr. Right's qualities might just help. For one, you'll discover a thing or two about your needs. Next, you can use the points to develop questions when "interviewing" the candidate later. Based on my criteria, for instance, I'd ask my prospective doctor if he's an expert in his specialty, and I'd confirm he wouldn't get agitated if I sought a second opinion.

My Dream Doctor...

1. Treats me as an individual and doesn't cookie-cut me into a plan that works for him. After all, I have to live with the plan twenty-four hours a day. If I am not in

"spin" doctor; she gives hope, while at the same time, she's straight about the future.

Hang in There until You Find a Match

Thinking about the ideal doctor is different from actually finding one: When we feel sick, the last thing we want to do is drag ourselves from doctor to doctor until we locate a match. Insurance plans are complicated and often restrict which specialists we can see. And, because of the preauthorization system of many HMOs,

agreement, the treatment won't work.

2. Is never threatened if I want to seek a second opinion. A second opinion does not question a doctor's intelligence; it simply gives patients confirmation they are on the right track.
3. Speaks to me as an equal. Not "I-am-the-doctor-you-are-the-patient—therefore-I-am-the-boss."
4. Looks at me in the eye when he is speaking.
5. Employs a staff that is professional, organized, and pleasant.
6. Is an expert in his specialty.
7. Is reliable and on time.
8. Makes the effort to make me feel comfortable when examining me or talking about personal or embarrassing issues.
9. Understands that this is my fifteen minutes to address my healthcare issues, so he doesn't take phone calls or have a hand on the doorknob while talking to me.
10. Validates, holds my hand, allows me to grieve when sharing bad news.
11. Provides me with the educational material, Web sites, or books to better understand my condition.
12. Can see me within a few weeks, not a few months, of calling to make an appointment.

by the time we get permission to visit certain doctors, we feel so lucky we want to stop right there. (This is kind of like accepting a less-than-perfect date after a long dry spell: He's better than nothing! At least someone wants to go out with me!)

Despite such difficulties, it is important that you exhaust all avenues to ensure you receive the very best care. If you aren't satisfied with your treatment, see every specialist your insurance allows until you find someone who works for you. A good idea is to ask your fellow patients about their practitioners. If someone you trust raves about her physician, find out if she is available under your insurance plan. It might also be worth researching the best in your area, despite insurance restrictions. You could potentially go out of plan and fight for care by this doctor, or opt to pay out of pocket. I have found that you can sometimes work with your insurance company to pay a portion of the cost. This approach is easier to manage if you negotiate with your insurance company before going to the doctor.

Forking out cash is tough, but this is the harsh reality of living with a chronic illness. And isn't your health worth it? In the United States, we have the finest healthcare in the world, despite its pitfalls. Take advantage of this fact. You have a right to seek out the very best.

The Questions to Ask

Now that you've found the right doctor, it's important to get the most out of your visits by asking pointed questions. Too often, if you don't ask, they won't tell. Going to the doctor requires gleaning a lot of information in a short amount of time, often in a hurried environment. I suggest you write out your questions and prioritize them. By getting prepared, you can rapid-fire your inquiries during the visit, and you'll be able to take good notes, comfortable you aren't forgetting anything.

A quick note: Be sure you save the right questions for the right healthcare provider. If your particular illness requires a special type of diet, for instance, instead of asking your transplant surgeon how to best prepare the food, check in with your specialist, the nutritionist, or dietitian. During the office visit, be sure to ask the following:

What's Your Number?—Sometimes I forget to ask the simplest questions, but, if an emergency comes up, these answers can be the most important. Ask your doctor the best way to contact her if you have questions between visits—by phone, e-mail, or fax. Write down her contact information. Find out if she has an assistant or partner who is more readily available. Ask who to call if you need a refill of a prescription, and make sure to get a number as well as a name.

What's Next?—I like to be optimistic, but I'm a realist, too. I feel better knowing what my options are if the current plan of treatment doesn't work. This tactic gives me the time to read up on alternatives. A few examples of questions might be: When should I expect a change in my symptoms due to the treatment plan? Will the changes happen gradually or suddenly? What happens if my condition gets worse? If I get better, how long will the treatment plan last? Are there any other therapies available if this one doesn't work?

What's an 'Emergency'?—When living with a chronic illness, feeling sick is a way of life, so sometimes it's hard to trust our body's signals. When we're always in pain, at what point is it a warning that we are in an emergency situation? Getting specific guidelines helps. For instance, if you struggle with high blood pressure, ask what blood pressure warrants a trip to the emergency room. Ask when a fever is a cause for alarm. If you're going into surgery, find out the signs of infection. If you have a catheter, learn what to do if it leaks. By getting specific responses to questions like these, you can plan ahead a little, and ease your mind.

Will You Take Good Care of Me?—If you are visiting the doctor prior to a new procedure or surgery, now's the time to get those last queries answered and to let the staff know what you need. Often the visit before a new course of treatment can be frightening. I find I'm comforted by asking questions like these:

- How long have you been doing this?
- Is there another patient I can speak to

who has had the procedure?
- It would be very helpful if someone would hold my hand during the procedure. Would that be possible?
- Will I feel any pain?
- Will you tell me what is going on during the procedure?
- Are there blankets available if I become cold?
- Will you tell my family how I am doing?

Such questions accomplish two things. First, they make you feel you are a true partner in your care. Next, they let your health team know how they can best help you. In my experience, too often we expect our care providers to read our minds. Also, don't ask these questions just before the procedure. Give your healthcare professionals time to respond to your requests.

Is There Anything I Need to Know About My Meds?– When you take medications, there can often be side effects. Ask your doctor if there is anything you should be on the look out for. Find out when to take the medication and whether to take it on a full or empty stomach. Be sure to ask if the medication will make you drowsy. When you pick up your meds, the pharmacist is also knowledgeable about medications and side effects.

The National Library of Medicine's Med-Line Plus, at www.nlm.nih.gov/medlineplus, is a great site to search for medication side effects. Also remember alcohol and medications don't always mix, be aware of this and read the label before taking. Useful tip: If you are on several meds at once, as most of us are, dosage schedules and amounts are easy to get mixed up. To eliminate uncertainty when discussing your medications, prepare a list of meds you're taking prior to the visit—or better yet, put them in a bag and take them with you.

How Bad (or Good) Is It, Really?—I have found if I set my sight on the right expectations, I do not get upset. The more up-front a doctor is about the possible outcomes of a treatment, the more realistic my expectations will be. This process wasn't always easy for me. Aligning my hopes with the truth was a skill I had to learn. When I was younger and on dialysis, despite what the specialists said, I thought all my problems would be solved once my name came up on the transplant list. "Once I'm off dialysis, I'll *really* live!" I'd think. I avoided the very real possibility that even if I underwent the surgery, the kidney could reject. After my second failed transplant, I realized I needed to reframe my expectations. There was no magic elixir that would just take the illness away. It was high time I started living for today, even if that meant being on dialysis.

Good physicians will push you to face reality when you don't necessarily want to know how bad something is. As another example, for many years, my doctors suspected my bone density was low, and they continually pushed me to take the test. I put it off and joked, "Thank God I'm not even five feet tall! If I fall, there's no way I'll break any bones when I'm this close to the ground."

At their prodding, I finally had the test and my bone density is indeed low, mainly from years of dialysis and the daily steroids. With their help, I've come out of denial, and I've researched the many treatments and exercises available. Now I realize I have lots of options to improve the condition.

Can I Get a Pamphlet on That?—In most cases, by simply asking your healthcare professional for printed material, you can receive ample information to begin the process of educating yourself.

If You Don't Like What You Hear, Get a Second Opinion

As you ask your questions and listen to the doctors' answers, remember you are never "stuck" with any one doctor's assessment of your situation. Like all of us, doctors make mistakes, or they draw different opinions based on the facts in front of them. You won't hurt her feelings (well, you might, but if you do, then she's not the one for you). Getting a second opinion can help confirm a diagnosis, or it can give you some wiggle room to pursue a new avenue of treatment.

A second opinion can also lift your spirits, as it did my friend Melissa's. Her doctor projected that she had two years before she would likely reject her kidney, which she received fifteen years ago. Melissa is a case manager for a healthcare company, so she's used to navigating the difficult waters of the medical field, but it seemed she had forgotten how to advocate for herself. She was resigned and depressed and hadn't even considered getting a second opinion from her transplant physician. I suggested to Melissa that she schedule an appointment. "You never know, he may have some new scoop on how to prevent chronic rejection," I said.

Melissa may end up hearing the same prognosis from the transplant team, but after she made the appointment she said she still felt better. She was taking back control and gained a sense of accomplishment because she knew she was pursuing all her resources.

Second opinions can also help you avoid the worst-case scenario: finding out, after the fact, that there was something you could have done to remedy the problem. Thank goodness Richard Daggett sought a second opinion. Diagnosed with polio at age thirteen, Daggett has spent his life monitoring the debilitating aftereffects of his disease.

Several years ago, Daggett visited his physician for a cold. "The doctor did some superficial tests and said, 'You're fatigued, go home and get some rest,' " Daggett recalls. "But I knew enough about polio and respiratory inhibition that I knew something wasn't right. I knew

Progress begins with the belief that what is necessary is possible.

—Norman Cousins

the residuals of polio left me with weakened lungs. I decided to call a pulmonary specialist. When I described my symptoms, they said, 'Come in as soon as you can.' It turns out I was suffering from pulmonary failure. I was admitted to the hospital. If I had taken the advice of my family physician, I probably would have died."

Trust Your Instincts (Or Save the Rooster Combs!)

Though we wish they did, doctors don't always know best. I'll never forget the time I landed in the emergency room after my knee conked out. My specialist recommended I go to the emergency room to get a test done so she could see if I'd torn my meniscus disk. This bout of trouble came on the heels of five weeks of drug therapy involving an expensive new med made of, believe it or not, rooster combs.

After the usual excruciating wait in the emergency room, the doctor finally saw me. I was in a tremendous amount of pain. I resisted my first instinct, which was to ask for a pain injection just to get out of my misery. After a quick examination, the doctor made the obvious observation that my knee was swollen. Without telling me her plans, she instructed the nurse to prepare a table where she could drain the excess fluid.

Once I realized what was happening, I explained to the nurse that the doctor should page my knee specialist to confer, since I didn't think she would approve of the procedure. And, hey! I didn't want my expensive rooster combs going down the drain!

The doctor wasn't too happy with my assertiveness, but I explained to her as nicely as I could that I've survived my chronic illness because I take control of my medical care, even when I'm in severe pain or I may need to inconvenience someone.

The doctor finally paged my specialist, who, as I suspected, recommended against removing the fluid. She instead suggested I get some crutches and hobble into her office the following morning.

A big part of me—the part that was in pain—wanted the emergency-room doctor to just make my knee better instantly. But my instincts told me that the best thing for my health, in the long-term, would involve a longer and more painful process. As it turned out, my knee was back to normal in about five days. And the best part of all—I saved my expensive rooster combs!

Like me, Shirley Jones (no relation to the celebrity) trusts her instincts when it comes to her medical care. She had kidney failure and sought a new doctor after hers repeatedly sidestepped her questions about transplantation. "When I probed my doctor about being placed on a transplant list, he would casually change the subject," she remembers. "The information (or lack of information) he was relaying was starting to take its toll on me emotionally. Doctors may know a lot about medicine, but they don't always know how to communicate the information you need." Rather than give in, Jones began researching her own condition. The search was fruitful and led her to much better care. "I read as much information as I could get my hands on and found a support group of fellow patients. I managed to get my own appointment with the transplant team and was listed with no help of my previous doctor," she explains. "I then found a doctor who was willing to participate in the day-to-day care of my transplant and be a true partner in my care. Today, I have a successful kidney/pancreas transplant."

Remember, when you have a chronic illness, your goal isn't to win a popularity contest with the medical staff. It's to get the best treatment available so you can live as healthy a life possible. You are the customer. You are employing these people and paying them for their services. Trust your instincts, and you will get the best care.

GOING SOLO

Researching on Your Own

Stretching beyond the hospital community to research can be a vital part of your healing process. By keeping up with the latest studies, alternative treatments, and news about your illness, you'll find you can reclaim some control over your health. More than once patients' own research has led to their involvement in cutting-edge research programs or successful use of alternative therapies. Also, researching can provide you with a meaningful and empowering project while your illness keeps you from other activities in your life.

The Internet

Just ten years ago, independent research entailed heading to the library and conducting a painstaking search

A MAP TO THE INTERNET: *Where Do You Want to Go?*

 It's easy to get lost in the infinitely layered world of the Web. According to the Patient's Guide to Healthcare Information on the Internet, there are about twenty thousand medical sites on the Internet.[2]

To avoid information overload, it helps to have a map, or a game plan of where you want to go. Are you interested in basic information on your condition? Start at a medical research site, like Medem at www.medem.com. This site gets its information from the nation's leading medical societies and offers libraries, news, and learning centers. Are you looking for a place to tell your story or to hear other people's? Start at www.healingwell.com. Are you looking for objective, comprehensive, newsy coverage on your illness? Do a search on a news site, like www.pbs.com, which put together a series on chronic illness in America. Oftentimes news outlets are a great resource since the information is nonjargony, more objective, and heavily researched. Don't know where to begin? Go to www.yahoo.com or www.google.com and type in a keyword. Here are a few good places to start, depending on your need.

U.S. Department of Health and Human Services—This is a searchable site that tells you everything you need to know about the HHS, a federal agency that helps protect

through hundreds of books, magazines, and newspaper articles—often yielding not-enough information. Today those of us with home computers can call up *too much* material in just a few seconds without leaving our homes.

What people find on the Internet can have a dramatic impact on their quality of care. Stephen Cattier was ini-

the general public's health, and, in specific, aids the elderly, the very young, the poor and the disabled with medical and insurance issues; available at www.os.dhhs.gov.

National Institutes of Health—Here you'll be able to look up medical conditions, medications, find out how you can participate in research studies, get references, look up information on the government's special health programs, and, well, the list goes on and on; available at www.nih.gov.

Medem—This site provides information from the nation's medical societies; available at www.medem.com.

The Patient's Guide to Healthcare Information on the Internet—This is a clearinghouse site that compiles the medical resources on the Internet and organizes them for you; available at www.patientsguide.com.

Healing Well—This easy-to-navigate site provides support, information, and resources on chronic illness; available at www.healingwell.com.

The Combined Health Information Database—This is a searchable database created by the federal government's health-related agencies. It is updated four times a year and lists education materials and program descriptions not indexed elsewhere on the Web; available at http://chid.nih.gov.

The Invisible Disabilities Advocate—This homegrown site helps people understand chronic illness; available at www.invisibledisabilities.com/websites.htm.

tially diagnosed with depression and anxiety, followed by a diagnosis of schizophrenia. When drugs for these ailments made his condition worse, Cattier began researching his symptoms on the Internet, reaching out to faraway doctors and connecting with other patients. He eventually discovered he had a series of allergies to agents like wheat, cow's milk, eggs, and dust mites. His research helped him to avoid the allergens and work with his doctors to fine-tune his treatment. Cattier continues to use the Internet to seek out new doctors, health studies, and information.

If you don't have access to the Internet, your local library probably offers Internet connections and free introductory classes. Check its schedule for information. The Internet is not difficult to use, so you may not need a class. Just ask a librarian how to get started and he or she will most likely be willing to help.

On-Line Support Systems

For many people the Internet fulfills an even more important need than fact gathering: emotional support. It is filled with message boards and chat rooms dedicated to chronic illness. Most illness-specific sites also have "community" sections where people can share their stories, respond to other people's comments, give advice, and exchange resources and information.

The benefits of an on-line support group are many. For one, you don't have to get out of your jammies to attend. The postings are anonymous, available around the clock, and you have the potential to meet people all over the world who share a common bond.

Mandy Gordon, who suffers from chronic fatigue syndrome, found a friend through the Internet who helped her cope with her loneliness. "We have met twice now and it's been great. It takes some of the weight off," she explains. "She has a similar problem so she's knows what it's like to not want to get out of bed."

The Internet Isn't Always Right

The Internet isn't a panacea. In fact, it must be used with great caution. First and foremost, do not believe everything you read on the Web. You will quickly discover there are a lot of people who post messages on boards or in chat rooms who are actually selling the latest snake oil. Some boards are monitored to limit these kinds of messages, but some unscrupulous e-mails manage to get posted. You'll also read amazing stories about people recovering from various ailments by using alternative medicines or methods. I would never discourage exploring all healthcare options, but such postings tend to get people's hopes up, and the results aren't always miraculous. Remember that anybody can put anything on the Web. Also, be sure to guard your privacy carefully—do you really know who is on the other end of that e-mail address? There are many examples of Internet crime and fraud, much of which is targeted to people who are not experienced Web users.

Never trust a computer you can't throw out a window.

—Steve Wozniak

There are ways to make sure the information you read is credible. First, did the author cite his or her source material? Do the citations check out? Are the sources reliable? Does the author or Webmaster list his or her contact information?

Another way to protect yourself is to look for the blue and red HONcode seal. The Health on the Net Foundation, or HON as it is widely known, created a code of ethics for medical Web developers. Those sites that adhere to its guidelines carry the seal. It is self-regulatory, though, so this system isn't foolproof. To find out more about HON's ethics, go to www.hon.ch.

Discuss what you learn on the Internet with your physician. Doctors are used to patients inquiring about information learned on the Internet. A good physician will comment fairly on any information you bring.

Libraries

While your local public library is a good place to start researching, be sure you don't forget about all the libraries in your area. If you live near a university or medical center, these may be even better options for

43

the type of digging you'll be doing. Often these have the most up-to-date medical books and periodicals. No matter where you choose to begin, be sure to use the libraries' finest resource: librarians. Getting librarians on your side can get you better information, faster, than the Internet. Don't be afraid to ask for their help—more often than not, they'll love the research challenge.

Periodicals

You'd be surprised at the wealth of information in newsletters, often put out by one or two dedicated people from a home office. These usually report local news about your illness, including support group listings and the latest goings on in the community. Since patients often develop the material, I've found these small desktop-published periodicals to carry information most pertinent to me. The other benefit of newsletters is you don't have to actively hunt down the information. It arrives in your mailbox once a month (or thereabouts). Research doesn't get much easier than that. Check with your local chronic illness foundation for area newsletters and information on how to subscribe.

Many diseases have their own weekly, monthly, or quarterly publications, such as the *Diabetic Digest* or the American Association of Kidney Patient's *aakpRENALIFE*. Check the Internet, the library, or ask at your doctor's office for a publication that's appropriate for you. With their insightful articles from patients and physicians, these magazines can be great, especially if you are bedridden and it's difficult for you to actively go out and do your own research.

PARTNERING WITH OTHERS
Educate Yourself through Support Groups

As you work with your medical care team and do your own research, you will run across literally hundreds of support groups for your disease. These can be a great way to get information, and they have the added benefit of helping you realize you aren't alone in this, that lots of people live with your chronic condition.

I have benefited from support groups. I have made great friends, felt understood, and learned new information on kidney disease—even though I thought I had already learned all there was to know! Penny Day, who suffers from chronic obstructive pulmonary disease (COPD), said she didn't really understand the disease until she joined a support group called the Emphysema Foundation for Our Right to Survive.

"The doctors don't really explain it; they just give you medication and that's it," Day explains. "Then I just happened to come across a support group called EFFORTS on the Internet. They are a wealth of information. Basically everything I learned about COPD I learned through them. I learned it's not a death sentence, and I learned how to have a better lifestyle. I don't think the medical community really understands what we are going through, and the people who are living with it obviously do."

Support groups not only offer members emotional support and camaraderie, but also practical solutions and ideas for living with a disability. Mandy Gordon, for example, discovered local yoga classes for people suffering from chronic fatigue syndrome through her on-line support group. This information was invaluable, as she had tried all other types of exercise, without success. "Even the most mild yoga left me exhausted, but this support group sent me a list of exercises [that did work] and where there are classes held," she says.

You can find support groups by looking on-line, asking your healthcare professional or your local hospital or nonprofit organization for your disease (such as the Lupus Foundation of America, if you have lupus).

OF HORSES AND SUPPORT GROUPS

A man inherited a horse. The horse had a remarkable thoroughbred heritage but was old and had seen better days. It had a very pronounced sway back and wheezed with every breath.

By some unusual twist of fate the new owner was able to get the tired old horse entered in the Kentucky Derby. Of course, the horse finished dead last. In fact it barely made the first turn by the time the winning horse crossed the finish line.

It came time for the Belmont Stakes, and the horse was entered in this race, too. Once again he finished last. Next came the Preakness Stakes. You guessed it, he was entered in the race. This time the horse barely made it out of the starting gate.

A friend of the owner asked him why he kept entering the horse in the races. "You know he can't win," he said.

"I realize that," explained the owner. "But I think he benefits from the association."

This is sort of like attending a support group. You are not going to experience a miracle cure. And it won't make all of your troubles go away. But you will meet people who are experiencing some of the same things you are—people who have worked together to develop coping skills and can help you learn some of these same skills. And, probably best of all, you will find people who can relate to your problems, people who genuinely care.

You may not win any races, but you will benefit from the association.

—Richard Daggett

Reprinted from the July/August 1992 Polio Survivors Newsletter, with permission from the author.

A Support Group in an Exercise Class' Clothing

I used to go to an exercise swimming program at the YMCA for people with arthritis. Every week a lively group of women would suit up and head to the pool. An exercise specialist from the Arthritis Foundation instructed us how to move our bodies appropriately so we would not injure our joints. Session after session, as we chatted and swam, the class naturally evolved into a support group. If the idea of an actual support group feels phony or unnatural to you, you can try joining an exercise group, or some other activity-related club for people with your illness, and you may just reap the benefits without the initial awkwardness. If you can't find one, consider starting your own.

Also a support group doesn't have to be a group of people; it can be a friend. When I was in my early twenties, I checked into the hospital to receive two units of blood, a procedure that occurred every six weeks. This particular day, I was placed in a room with a girl named Gloria. Gloria had lived with kidney disease for as long as I had. We became fast friends. If I hadn't have dozed off because of the sleeping medication, we could have chatted nonstop for six hours. Gloria and I exchanged phone numbers and continued our friendship. We would discuss symptoms over the phone at night, talk about solutions to daily problems, and listen to each other's stories of dating. A hot topic was when—or if— you tell a date you have an illness. The priceless conversations allowed me to talk openly with someone who understood.

Because I benefited so greatly from this experience, I decided to create the Renal Support Network Directory, a booklet of names and phone numbers of people with renal disease. I asked for patient volunteers to lend their names and phone numbers so others with renal disease would always have a friend to turn to. The first edition in 1993 had more than two hundred patients and family members. Today I am printing ten thousand copies of the seventh edition.

Pitfalls of Support Groups

Some groups can reinforce the "victim" role of having a chronic illness, and that's not what you want. In support groups, I've found I've met two types of people: those who are searching for solutions to their problems and those who are content to continually complain about their problems. When you visit a support group, if the majority of participants are negative and not trying to chart a new future for themselves, run for the hills!

One group I joined seemed intent on only exchanging horror stories about symptoms and medical professionals. While learning about other people's symptoms can be validating, even relieving, if all the talk is negative, negative, negative—beware. You can start to feel even worse because you are always dwelling on the pain. You can second-guess your care, and you can hold on to your anger because it resurfaces week after week. My suggestion is to always give a support group a few visits before making up your mind. But if it is persistently a downer, quit! Find another one that meets your needs.

A man too busy to take care of his health is like a mechanic too busy to take care of his tools.

—Spanish Proverb

DON'T GET DISCOURAGED

When You Get Overwhelmed by Your Research, Stop

However you go about your information gathering, I encourage you not to get discouraged. It's easy to become depressed after reading story after story of other people's tragic losses. It's only a matter of time before you start thinking, "Is this going to happen to me?" When you start to get overwhelmed, stop. Get offline or get out of the library and read an uplifting book, see a funny movie, or cuddle up with your cat. Do anything that gets your mind off your health, even if it's only for a few moments.

When you come across hard-to-swallow information, remind yourself of what is going right. The one thing that is truly inspiring about living with a chronic disease is how much hope is in our future. When I start to get down, I think of the thousands of people who are working behind the scenes inventing medication, treatment regimens or preventative measures to improve our lives. The medical field advances so quickly, it is hard to keep up on the latest and greatest. We never stop learning, so hang on to hope!

3

GRAB CONTROL OF YOUR MIND AND BODY

In these pages, you'll learn how your mind can be a powerful ally in regaining a sense of well-being. You'll also discover strategies to cope with your changing body so you can get through the bad days and stick with your diet and exercise programs.

The harder you're thrown, why the higher you bounce.

—Edmund Vance Cooke

L IVING WITH A chronic illness since the age of two, I became aware early on that I was different. For a long time, that sense of being different also made me feel as if I were broken. It took years of hard work and personal growth to finally see myself as a whole human being, rather than as damaged goods.

After talking to scores of individuals who have chronic illness, it's become apparent that my struggle with a dented self-image isn't unique. In fact, you're probably facing your own case of the "Damaged Goods Syndrome" right now. I'd love to tell you that once dealt with, the syndrome is gone for good. Unfortunately, it isn't. But you have the power to keep that ever-present negative self-talk in check.

As you learn to live with your illness, you'll discover that your mind can be your best friend. It can help you keep those Damaged Goods thoughts at bay, stay in charge of your health, and—many believe—heal your body. Your mind can also be your worst enemy: It can keep you locked in the Syndrome, reinforcing the thought that you aren't good enough, healthy enough, or worthy enough to live a full life.

The key here is that you make the choice. You choose to stay stuck, or you choose to free yourself from the mental anxiety that comes along with illness. In the following pages, I'm going to show you how to select the latter and make your mind the greatest ally as continue your journey with disease.

OVERCOMING THE DAMAGED GOODS SYNDROME
Identify the Trash ...

As I said, I believe we each have the power to control our thoughts, even the ones that are most troubling, worrisome, or self-defeating. Taking charge of what seems like a runaway train involves learning how to switch our negative thoughts to positive ones. This takes practice and diligence. The first step is to become your own personal inventory control specialist. Remember that old saying, "Garbage in, garbage out?" Apply it to your brain. Here are a few pieces of trash that may be in your bin. Any of these sound familiar?

Negative Self-Talk—This is that chatter in your head that says, "I'm not good enough," "What will everyone think?" or "If only I were healthier, prettier, smarter or [insert favorite self-destructive word here], then I would have a happy life." Often we're so used to saying these things to ourselves, we don't even recognize their droning negativity. "If only ..." is a dead-end road that prevents you from living your life to its fullest NOW. If you hear your mind saying "if only ..." redirect it. Remind yourself of something wonderful about you— what a good friend you are or how you made your neighbor smile this morning when you helped with her groceries.

Negative Media—Stay away from media that sets unrealistic expectations about how you should look, and what your life should be like (frolicking on the beach in the south of France, martini in hand). Life is too short to flip even one page of a magazine that tells you you're "less than" if you're not buffed like Arnold Schwarzenegger, or you're not Amazon-woman tall with a twenty-six-inch waist and a hunka-hunka burnin' love by your side. What would the world be like if everyone looked like the supposed ideal the media relishes? Bo-ring.

Negative Words from Others—You've probably noticed that not everyone knows how to be helpful as you negotiate your illness. Despite good intentions, many people simply reiterate the down side of your situation: "Oh, how awwwful that you're so sick," or "When will you get better?" There are also those who just won't treat you as an equal or view you as anything but Damaged Goods. Stop and think about who your best supporters are, regardless of who is around the most. Then minimize the time you spend with the negative or less helpful people, and focus more attention on those who give the genuine gift of friendship.

What kind of junk is filling up your head? Hunt it down, pick it up ...

... And Take It Out

Time to head for the dumpster! There are lots of ways you can replace those negative thoughts with positive ones. Just by saying a kind word or smiling at a passerby, you spread joy, and in the process squeeze out those "I'm-not-okay" messages. Remember, every time you send a self-deprecating thought to the compost heap, you're pulling out another chink of the Damaged Goods Syndrome's armor.

Read Inspiring Stories—I take strength from reading about people who have overcome great obstacles, and I learn valuable lessons by seeing how they did it. For this reason, *Chicken Soup for the Soul* books are among my favorite. I discovered another great read when I was in an airport on my way to Chicago. I was feeling depressed about my impending hysterectomy and was looking for a diversion. I was scanning the airport bookstore's newest arrivals, and staring back at me was Armstrong's *It's Not About the Bike*. As I said earlier, this inspiring story is about a remarkable man who not only overcame life-threatening cancer, but, shortly after, won the Tour de France. His upbeat, realistic writings were just what I needed to gain the courage to address my problem at hand. Lance lets his readers know that an illness is difficult, but doable. I could identify with him, even though I had never been a pro cyclist or dealt with advanced cancer. I share a belief with Armstrong: Anything is possible if you don't give up hope.

Laugh—You may not feel like it, but laughing can make your psyche and your body feel better. Several research studies have shown that a deep belly laugh can lower blood pressure,[1] reduce stress hormone levels,[2] and boost immune function.[3] It is also well documented that laughter minimizes pain.[4]

And as we all know, laughter creates an overall feeling of goodwill. So go to a movie or a comedy club, look at the world through a child's eyes, or attend a "laugh therapy" course—there are lots of ways to replant laughter in your life.

Humor has a serious side, too. It can help take the power away from your illness by stripping the embarrassment out of the many awkward situations sickness can bring up. Many years ago I had to resort to the wonderful world of wigs after I lost my hair due to multiple surgeries. (I never looked good in scarves; my head is just the wrong shape.) I was back to work after my time in the hospital, and I was desperately insecure about my new style; I prayed no one would notice. My boss, Eric, asked everyone to join him for lunch. We all piled in his Ford Blazer, and I rode shotgun.

One of my coworkers, Tim, reached for something in the visor in front of me, and his ring caught my wig. When he pulled his hand back, my wig went flying with it. I sat in the front seat, bald and mortified, cursing the fact I got out of bed that morning. But Tim, whose hair was a little thinner than mine, made a quick recovery. "Oh, wow," he said. "Can I borrow this? I could really use it." We all cracked up. Tim's self-deprecating crack broke the tension and made me feel one of the group, not the odd baldy out.

Seek Support from People Who Understand—Talking with real people who are in similar situations gives me encouragement and helps me to keep a clear perspective. Likewise, I'm able to vent fears and frustrations that might otherwise lie dormant. It's funny how just expressing your troubles to an attentive, empathetic listener can alleviate your anxiety and provide so much reassurance.

Pay Attention to What You Can Control—I've said it before, and I'll say it again. Dwelling on things over which you have no control is a recipe for disaster. Here's a simple exercise that helps me when I'm feeling overwhelmed: I write down the situation that is bothering me and, underneath, the actions I can take to improve it. If I can't write anything down, I realize I'm powerless over the problem, and I have to release it to faith, luck or patience. If I can do something, then my written words point me in a clear direction, where I know I'll get results.

Listen to Motivational Tapes—Motivational speakers are much like nonreligious ministers. They encourage peo-

A DINNER INVITATION FOR ONE: *Set a Place for You*

 Throughout my journey of self-discovery, I've read a lot of books. One was called *Intimate Connections* by Dr. David D. Burns. This book is about eliminating the negative thinking and low self-esteem that can cause loneliness and shyness.[6] I came upon it in my late teens, and one of its points has stuck with me all these years.

The author instructs readers to ask themselves the question, *When you come home from work, what do you generally do for dinner?*[7] Despite my genuine love of cooking, my answer to this question was, "Throw a turkey sandwich together, and it eat on the run!"

Dr. Burns then goes on to ask, *If you had people over for dinner, would you serve them something you*

ple to achieve their goals, whether in their profession, finances, health, or love. I often pop in a cassette while I'm in the car, as a way to endure what would otherwise be a frustrating encounter with rush-hour traffic. I've also turned to the voice of a favorite motivational speaker for encouragement during hospital stays. Each time I listen, I undoubtedly come away with more enthusiasm for life. Give it a try! Enthusiasm is contagious! These are three of my favorite speakers: Les Brown, Wayne Dyer, and Marianne Williamson.[5] Check their tapes out from the library; it certainly can't hurt.

Take Your Body Someplace Positive

Sometimes your mind lets you down. Despite all of your efforts to divert negative thinking, the bad thoughts continue their assault. At this point, I encourage you to

normally serve yourself?[8] For me, the answer was an unequivocal, "NO!" There was no way I would serve a guest a turkey sandwich on stale bread and ask her to wolf it down while standing at the counter. Nor would I heap a bowl of cottage cheese and say, "Bon appetite!" When I'd have someone over, I'd spend hours planning and cooking. I wouldn't do it for myself, though, because I simply wasn't worth it.

With the goal of improving the way you see yourself, Dr. Burns suggests you treat yourself like you'd treat a dinner guest. I have to confess I don't go to quite the extent that I do for company every night, but I have made some changes. I set a place for myself at the table (and my husband as well, if he behaves!), and I make the effort to create a healthy meal. *Having company for dinner tonight? Or is it just you?*

enact the "Take Your Body Someplace Positive, And Your Mind Will Follow" concept.

This boils down to forcing yourself to get out in the world, even if you don't want to. Have you ever noticed that when you push yourself to do something you don't really feel like doing, once you're doing it, you feel good about it? Perhaps it's getting dressed and driving thirty minutes to a friend's birthday party, attending a charity function, or simply embarking on some household task. You dread the idea of moving, but somewhere between leaving the couch and handing your friend her birthday present, you find you're glad you pushed beyond your initial resistance. Getting out and connecting with friends actually makes you feel better, mentally and physically.

The Magic of 'Acting as If'

But how do you get past that mental blockade that has you velcroed to the couch? Throughout my life with a chronic illness, there have been countless times I've wanted to stay in bed and feel sorry for myself, marinating in the Damaged Goods Syndrome. I've had to muster every ounce of my available energy, literally pick up my body, get dressed and force myself to move, take a walk, anything! As a part of this process, I rely heavily on the "Acting as If" concept. If you act as if something you want to be true is already true, there's a good chance that before you know it, you won't be acting any more. I act as if I have the energy for a walk, and even though I don't, once I'm out the door, I already feel revitalized. I act as if I can't wait to go to the birthday party, and before you know it I'm laughing with my friends.

I learned the technique from my Grandpa Joe. Grandpa Joe woke up one morning, felt ill, went to the hospital, and came home three days later blind from diabetes. He never knew he had diabetes until that hospital visit, which was his first ever. After he lost his eyesight, my grandpa never missed a beat. My earliest memory of Grandpa Joe was watching him make beautiful ceramics, many of which I still have today. When he wasn't creating his artwork, he would walk around the neighborhood for hours by himself, his cane leading his way. His senses became so honed on these walks, he could hear the ice cream truck before I could—and since I was in grade school, my ears were pretty sharp when it came to the ice cream truck. He even became fluent in Braille, which he picked up in his fifties.

I grew up thinking all blind men hand-sculpted art pieces, walked freely about the neighborhood, and read

Whether you think you can do a thing or think you can't do a thing, you are right.

—Henry Ford

58

books. Grandpa Joe's secret? He acted as if he could still see.

Helping Others Helps You

Volunteering and helping others fly in the face of the Damaged Goods Syndrome by confirming you still have something to offer despite your disease. Although it may feel like a huge undertaking at first, taking your mind off you and placing it selflessly on others can be to the soul as water is to the thirsty.

We've all heard the saying, "There's always somebody worse off than you." You come face to face with this truth when you reach out and help someone else. I can honestly say I have never volunteered and felt worse for the effort.

My friend Heather Powell was diagnosed with kidney failure when she was eight years old. Through her parent's involvement, she began volunteering as a young child. "I became the poster child for the Kidney Foundation," she recalls. After earning her master's degree later in life, the only work Heather wanted to do was to assist others like her. "I knew that was where my heart was. I knew where these people were coming from and that I could help them beyond the social work aspect. I could help because I had lived it," she said.

Heather now works as the program director for the Arkansas Kidney Foundation. She recommends volunteer work to anyone with chronic illness. "Any time you get out there and volunteer, you always see you're not the only one with problems. And if you can help someone, it only makes you feel better."

Cynthia Perkins is another person who has built a life around aiding other people, despite living with several illnesses. She worked as a secretary before she was diagnosed with fibromyalgia, chemical sensitivity and chronic fatigue syndrome. Unable to return to the same workplace, Cynthia went back to school and got her bachelor's degree in psychology and a master's degree in counseling. After graduating, she began a phone- and instant-messaging-based consultation business, aimed at counseling people struggling with their own chronic conditions.

"It took me nine years to get my degrees. When I finished my health had deteriorated completely, and I was not able to go back to work in any environment; that is when I set up my Internet business. For me it is more about nourishing my soul through contributing information to the world that is not readily available, as well as giving and the satisfaction that comes from that."

You may be asking yourself, "What can I do? My energy level is so low I can barely take care of myself." To that I reply, "Volunteer your ear!" So often the greatest gift you can give to another person is to simply listen. That's all many people need to gain the strength to make a difficult decision or to make it through the day. It doesn't matter if you feel inadequately trained to solve the person's problem. I heard someone say once, "People don't care how much you know, until they know how much you care." If you *care*, you don't need more expertise than that.

HEALING YOUR BODY IMAGE

Move Past the 'Dings'

Part of living with the Damaged Goods Syndrome is recognizing your body has a few dings. After thirty-five surgeries to date, I have more than just a few dings. I joked for years that I've never been older than the number of surgeries I've had! Now that I'm thirty-five, I guess it's time to retire that joke.

Since kidney disease stunted my growth, I'm short, not even five feet. While some people may think this is "cute," my size has caused me a lot of image problems.

For one, people treated me as though I were a child far into adulthood. And for many years, I had a hard time being taken seriously. This was difficult, since I desperately *needed* to be taken seriously. I had ideas and career plans and important things to say, but I'd just get a pat on the head and a, "That's nice, Lori." So I devised a plan. I went on a mission to discover the things I loved to do and then I vowed to *become an expert* in those areas. If I excelled, I reasoned, I'd gain my peers' respect—and perhaps a few metaphorical inches. And you know what? It worked. Today I often say, "I am taller than I look." And so it is with you!

Life is 10 percent what you make it and 90 percent how you take it.

—Irving Berlin

Key to my plan was taking aim at areas where I *could* excel. I didn't choose to become a pro volleyball player for a reason. Until they change the rules and make the ball go under the net, I will never have a future in that sport. So why set myself up for failure? I zeroed in on public speaking, organizing events, educating my peers and healthcare workers—all of which I can do despite my small size—and all of which give me much personal satisfaction.

What skills can you become an expert in, despite your body's limitations?

Get Pleasure from Activities Your Body CAN Do

This concept works on a recreational scale as well. Perhaps you're great at crossword puzzles, or you love to bird watch. Do activities that give you pleasure, rather than ruminating over what your body can't do anymore.

My passion is crafts. I've been a craft addict since my teens. I made so many items in my youth, in fact, I started taking the surplus with me during my regular trips to the hospital. Surprisingly, many nurses asked me if I would sell my creations. Never one to turn down a business opportunity, I agreed. This began a very

A SHAVE AND A HAIRCUT: *Battle the Body Image Blues*

 One of the greatest challenges of living with a chronic illness is accepting the changes in your physical appearance. Your hair may thin or your skin may break out due to the medication you're taking. You may gain or lose weight rapidly. You may carry scars because of surgery. You may walk with a limp because of arthritis, or you may need a wheelchair to get around.

With such ever-present visual reminders of your condition, it's easy to start hating your body. The following suggestions aren't going to change your world, but they'll help a little bit—and on those bad days, a little can help *a lot.*

Get the Best Wig or Scarf Money Can Buy—If your hair thins or starts to fall out, spend as much money as it takes to get a head covering that makes you feel comfortable. If you don't feel comfortable, you won't go out, and if you hibernate, you isolate—a quick way to get an unbeatable case of the blues.

Honor Your Scars—Every scar has a story, and for people with chronic disease, oftentimes the story is about how the procedure that left the scar saved your life. Love your scars for what they represent, rather than hating them for how they look. Honor them by rubbing them with lotion (after they have healed) or vitamin E. Get used

peculiar situation. I would be admitted to the hospital, and I would bring beaded holiday ornaments, painted T-shirts, and an array of country crafts. I'd set them out for show on the table by my bed. If I was sleeping, the display worked on the honor system. Many times I woke up with checks in my nightstand for items nurses

to feeling the rough edges or the bumpy skin. It may be difficult at first to see your scars in this new light, but it becomes easier with practice.

Dress Up—To combat the temptation to get down and stay there, I make it a habit to dress up occasionally or at least wear something besides my robe, sweats or other "icky" clothes.

Put on Makeup or Shave—For women, a little makeup, especially blush, can do wonders. For men who normally shave, keep it up! If you indulge in a little vanity, you'll look better, which will make you feel better, too.

Salon Treatment—I remember many days when my greatest desire was to stay in my jammies and leave my hair a matted mess. Instead, I would force myself to get my hair cut and blown dry, and either paint my own nails or treat myself to a massage or a professional manicure and pedicure. It's amazing how comforting such pampering can be, thanks to the magical healing power of human touch.

Say Self-Affirmations—These short, uplifting phrases can do wonders for your spirit—if you believe in them. Their secret lies in the power of positive thinking. Any bookstore offers an array of phrase-packed booklets. In the meantime, try out some of these: "I love and appreciate myself just as I am." "Everyday in every way I am getting better and better." "I have the ability to create what I want in my life."[9]

had bought on their break. With this money, I reinvested in the art therapy I so desperately needed.

Whether I was really talented, I'll never really know. The reality was I loved it, and I had a captive audience of nurses who liked to shop. Also, they probably understood that it was psychologically important for me that

KEEPING POSITIVE DURING HOSPITAL STAYS

One of the more frustrating aspects of living with a chronic illness is the hurry-up-and-wait syndrome. It happens nearly every time you have a medical appointment, not to mention when you land in the hospital. These waiting periods can have a gratingly negative impact on your self-esteem. You start to feel that since your time is wasted waiting, it must not be worth much. And if your time isn't worth much, then you must not be worth much. It's a real mental domino effect.

To combat this Damaged Goods thinking, I assemble my survival gear for those mundane hospital stays: books, a writing tablet, simple art projects, and stationery or thank you notes. Sometimes I'll take my laptop if I know my stay will be extended, and I expect to have the energy to work. It may be slow going, especially when I don't feel well, but as I write letters, or outline a presentation for work, I gain a keen sense of accomplishment and comfort, knowing that those hours in the hospital bed haven't been wasted.

I also make it a rule to keep the television off, unless I'm tuning into a particular program. Channel surfing can be depressing in the hospital, making you feel like your brain is numb. If I'm too worn down to work or write, I'll keep a few positive books by my side such as *How Much Joy Can You Stand* by Suzanne Falter-Barns.[10] I have felt so down during hospital stays, I have literally had to force myself to dip into my arsenal of distractions, and remind myself that in order to get through, I better Take My Body Someplace Positive. This is especially hard to do when you feel physically weak or have been prescribed bed rest, but pushing yourself is worth it. I've found by Taking My Body Someplace Positive, I've turned even the worst days into passable days—and that's no small accomplishment.

they bought my wares. Even today when I visit, veteran nurses ask me, "What are you selling today?"

The Power of Visualization

Not only do you have the power to create a positive attitude, I believe you also have the power to heal aspects of your broken body. I'm not suggesting everyone is able to think or pray their illnesses away, but there is strong evidence that suggests people have more control over their well-being than the medical community or our culture currently accepts.

For centuries people have believed the mind has the capacity to heal. Navajo Indians used imagery to encourage ill people to "see" themselves as healthy. Ancient Egyptians and Greeks believed that visualization released spirits in the brain, which stimulated the heart and other parts of the body.[11]

Whether or not such methods work from a physiological perspective, if you are open to them, they may be worth a try. They are easily applied to people living

A MINIMASSAGE FOR THE MIND: *Silence the Clutter!*

 Even if you don't believe visualization has the power to heal, it can still help you. Sometimes our minds are so cluttered living with the dailies of a chronic illness, it's important to step back and clear our heads. Using mind techniques can shift your thoughts away from the despair, fear, and anxiety that can go hand-in-hand with chronic illness. Dr. Wayne Dyer, a psychotherapist, author, and motivational speaker suggests this exercise, which I've paraphrased for simplicity:

Picture a basketball digital scoreboard. Once you have a strong visual of the scoreboard, picture a score of twenty-four. Slowly visualize the scoreboard counting backward—twenty-three, twenty-two, twenty-one, etc. Focus your mind only on the score. If another thought comes to your mind you have to start again.

I never could get past the number sixteen without thinking about something else, but the first time I tried I only went to twenty-two. I got better with practice.

Relaxation exercises like these aren't long-term fixes. They're simply minimassages for the mind that will help you quiet your thoughts so you can breathe through the really tough days.

with chronic illness, and lots of hospitals are beginning to introduce visualization therapies, especially for people with cancer. The psychological and spiritual benefits alone may make it worthwhile. Ask your doctor if she can recommend supplemental therapies that include visualization, or do a little research on the Internet or your local library to find more information.

Visualization is one tool you can use to gain control of your illness, but it's not a cure all. Keep your expectations real, and don't abandon your doctor, medication, or treatment plan.

Turning It over to God

Where there is sickness, there is prayer. The two seem to go hand-in-hand. But why? Anecdotal evidence of medical miracles inspired by prayer abound on the Internet, and hundreds of books have been written on the relationship between prayer and healing.

I believe in a higher power, which I choose to call God. My family and I have prayed many times before surgery. When I am sick, friends often tell me they are praying for me, and it brings me comfort. So praying is a part of my life.

What I feel about prayer is irrelevant. It is something that is so personal, you have to check in with your spiritual self and decide if it is something that will be helpful to you.

For many, prayers are useful simply because they impart peace and calm. For me, praying is the ultimate way to let go of things that are not in my control. Praying reminds me that someone else is in charge, an idea that I desperately need when my illness is at its worst. It's not surprising, then, that the Serenity Prayer is one of my favorites: "God grant me the serenity to accept the things I cannot change, the courage to change the things I can, and the wisdom to know the difference."

TAKING CARE OF OUR BODIES

Diet and Exercise, Ugh

Here comes the broken record! We hear so much about diet and exercise, it seems that everyone who's had his fifteen minutes of fame has written a book on the subject. My thoughts are nothing splashy or profound. They entail just a few management ideas particular to living with physical limitations. When you have a chronic illness, your diet and exercise ideals may differ greatly from the mainstream's. Each particular illness seems to carry its own diet and exercise guidelines, and I know that adhering to these can be the most daunting of tasks.

Staying on Track with a Restrictive Diet

Frankly, I hate the word "diet." I prefer to think of it as healthy eating, unless of course you're where I've often been, with kidney failure and on dialysis. In that case, you're not supposed to eat many of the foods that are normally good for you—particularly anything containing potassium, like many fruits and vegetables. Even though the diet rules you've been given are for your own good, it is easy to become disheartened and subsequently obsessed with the foods you cannot have. Here are some ideas to keep you motivated:

Distract Yourself during Craving Times—I work on crafts or beading at night, the time I am most likely to crave the foods I can't have. If you find yourself craving certain foods at, say, three o'clock, get up from your desk, take a walk, and get a drink of water.

Turn down the Television, Or Turn It Off—Ever notice how many television commercials are for tantalizing food? And those mouth-watering images are always of something that's a no-no for you! Turning the volume down during program breaks is one way to steer clear of temptation. Another solution is to turn the tube off altogether.

Eat When You're Hungry—I have also found it helpful to stay mindful of when I'm starting to get hungry—and eating then—instead of waiting until I'm famished.

Once I'm really hungry, it's tough to think straight enough to stick to my restrictions.

CAN WE ADD A LITTLE COMPASSION TO THE MENU?

You can probably relate when I say my diet is very difficult. Anyone who can adhere to it deserves some sort of medal of honor for self-control. Sometimes healthcare professionals forget how hard it is, and they make you feel bad when you aren't compliant. I think it's important for them to validate patients' frustrations about sticking to a near-impossible diet, rather than admonishing them to get with the program: "You're noncompliant. You gained too much fluid today." Hearing this makes me want to shout, "Well, when it's 105 degrees outside, you try not drinking when you're thirsty!"

In my book, "noncompliant" is not the correct word. It implies you're doing something wrong, when in fact, it's very human to eat and drink what your body craves. What would be helpful is for healthcare professionals to say, "I know how tough this is," rather than pretending that avoiding anything with potassium isn't all that hard, or that it's fun to say good-bye forever to chocolate or many fruits.

"Hey, can we get a little *compassion* over here?"

Stockpile Good Foods—It also seems to make life a little easier when I have ready-access foods available for times when I'm really bugged. I suggest keeping allowed foods prepared and ready in the fridge or cupboard for quick relief during weak moments.

Get Permission to Cheat—Why not ask your doctor or nutritionist for permission to cheat on your diet once in a while? Sometimes the flexibility to color outside the lines on special occasions can offer a bit of emotional relief and remind us that the simple pleasures of life can still be ours, even when we have a chronic illness.

Experiment with Different Recipes—There are a variety of Web sites and books that have tempting recipes that will meet your nutritional requirements. A good place to start is the Kitchen Link at www.kitchenlink.com. This is a compilation site that links to all things cooking related on the 'Net. It has hundreds of sections, including healthy eating, diabetic recipes, sugar-free recipes, and recommended foods for people with milk allergies. There is also a search engine, where you can plug in a food and up will pop its nutritional bio, including calories and fat content.

Make Exercise Fun

As for exercise, I have to admit I rather hate that word, too! I tend to agree with Mark Twain when he said, "Every time I feel the urge to exercise, I lie down until it goes away."

That's not to say I don't love to play—like dancing 'til I drop or joining a good game of badminton. It's the thought of going to the gym to *exercise* that isn't very appealing.

In my opinion, keeping motivated to stay fit is ten times more difficult for people living with chronic disease. Why? For starters, even "fun" exercise is painful—if I dance all night, my knees are inevitably swollen and sore the next day. Next, we have some days where it's nearly impossible to get out of the house, let alone go to the track.

I push through by remembering the benefits of moving my body. Many studies have shown the link between exercise and healing, and quite a few books have been written on the subject.

In their book *Healing Moves*, Carol and Mitchell Krucoff explore the idea that "Simple exercise can have profound healing affects."[12] They look at the latest scientific findings about exercise's therapeutic

I can't change the direction of the wind, but I can adjust my sails to always reach my destination

—Jimmy Dean

70

power and present a program to help treat medical conditions including diabetes, depression, asthma, arthritis, high cholesterol, heart disease, osteoporosis, and cancer.

Like me, the Krucoffs suggest making exercise an adventure by swimming, playing tennis, doing martial arts—any activity that makes you view it as a "play break" rather than a chore. The Krucoffs explain:

> Our theme is that, in many ways, movement is an ideal medicine. It's extremely effective, free (or at least inexpensive), low risk, abundantly available, socially acceptable and simple to do. When compared to traditional treatments, such as drugs and surgery, the risk/benefit profile frequently is far superior. ... The time you spend moving is generally repaid in full by the energy, relaxation, and pleasure that physical activity brings. Daily movement is much more than a health responsibility, like brushing your teeth. It's a pleasurable, precious gift that people can give themselves. Taking thirty minutes each day to be present in your body, to breathe deeply, and to propel yourself through space is one of life's great joys, enriching body, mind and spirit.[13]

Even though I *know* what these guys are saying is true, it's still really hard to get out there and move several times a week. Here are some tips that help me:

Have a Good Time—As the Krucoffs suggest, do something you already love to do, and pursue it with childlike enthusiasm. Team sports are good options—remember how you used to play soccer? How about gardening? That's good exercise, too.

Swimming, table tennis, dancing, or riding a stationary bike while listening to a favorite CD also work for me. Be realistic, though, and follow any specific limitations on exercises recommended by your physician.

A PERMISSION SLIP TO DO NOTHING: *Yes, You're Allowed*

A worthy addition to your Toolbox is a permission slip bearing the words, "It's okay to do nothing!" So often we feel guilty for taking a step back, sitting down and simply being still for an hour or even a day.

We live in a society which pounds a continual drum beat, "Go for it! Get more done! Make hay before the sun shines!" It's easy to become so busy that we neglect to address the feelings and thoughts that are going on inside. I believe there's a happy medium between finding ways to remain vital, versus overdoing it at the expense of inner tranquility.

When living with a chronic illness, you get tired. The process is exhausting. Listen to your body, and when you need a rest, rest!

Create an Exercise Jar—This one comes from my dietitian. She suggested I think of something indulgent I would like to buy for myself, like perfume, jewelry, or a nice massage. Each time I keep my commitment to exercise, I place a dollar in the jar. When I reach the purchase amount, I reward myself by buying the item.

Join a Team—Join a bowling league, for instance. This is a way to meet new friends and get a little physical activity in the process. If you can't bowl or have a physical limitation (such as back trouble), go to socialize and get out of the house. Your job can be to cheer on your favorite team.

Make an Exercise Date—When I'm chatting with a friend, I usually forget that I'm exercising. Meeting someone at a specific time and place also holds me accountable to someone other than myself, which makes me keep the date.

Exercise tips are helpful, but they don't always provide the needed motivation to spur you into action. I personally get pumped up by hearing real peoples' testimonials of how they beat the odds. So I'll end this chapter with my friend Bryon Vouga's remarkable story. In 1999, thirty-year-old high school teacher Vouga decided to ride his bike from Huntington Beach, California, to Jacksonville, Florida. He wouldn't be the first rider to make the trek, but he was the first who was hemodialysis-dependent with kidney failure. "I want to put a human face on kidney disease," Vouga said at a rally before he set out on the 2,375 mile journey. "I am using my cross-country trip to prove to myself and others that we do not have to be 'victims' of kidney disease, dialysis treatment, or anemia."

Vouga's struggle with kidney disease began when he was sixteen, after he was diagnosed with the glomerulonephritis, a condition that causes chronic renal failure. He's had two unsuccessful kidney transplants and, until his recent successful transplant, he had been on hemodialysis for more than ten years. Despite Vouga's poor health, his dream had always been to cycle across the country. That meant staying in shape, even during hospital stays.

> One time when I was in the hospital trying to recover from one of the operations, I had to get out and exercise. There was a nurse's station in the middle of the floor. I couldn't walk by myself because I was attached to so many IV poles. My friends, family, and I would walk around the nurse's station as many times as possible so I could build up my strength each day. My hair was always a mess so I would wear a cycling cap. Sometimes I would close my eyes and envision I was riding a bike instead of being in a hospital.

Vouga took his nephrology nurse on his cross-country trip to monitor his health; his aunt and uncle followed along to prepare compliant foods. The day he left for the journey, he said, "Today this is the beginning of my victory ride."

On July 26, Vouga reached his final destination of Jacksonville, Florida. He symbolized the end of his trek by dipping his bike into the Atlantic Ocean. Today he is married, has received a successful third transplant, and has a child. He continues to stay fit riding his bike and plans to bike across Australia someday.

Like Vouga, you can reach your goals, fitness and otherwise. What would you like to do that you've always dreamed of? Today could be the first day of *your* victory ride!

4

WHAT TO DO ABOUT WORK

You've survived the doctor visits, the diagnoses, the prodding exams. You've made it through the loss and the grief and accepted that today, right now, you feel as good as you're going to feel. Now's the time to step out of survival mode and into living mode. In this and the next chapter, you'll discover how to do the things you used to do, like resuming work and (yes!) having fun.

Let us realize that the privilege to work is a gift, that power to work is a blessing, that love of work is success.

—David O'McKay

PATRICIA HARRIMAN HAS lived with chronic fatigue syndrome and fibromyalgia for fourteen years. During this time she has suffered irritable bowel syndrome, panic attacks to the point of being homebound, dizzy spells, which make it impossible for her to drive, and depression. Prior to getting sick at age thirty-seven, she described herself as "strong" and "energetic."

"At first I was so terribly sad," she recalls. "My life had been taken from me. I grieved for my old self. And then I learned to let go and accept. Just accept. It is what it is." From that place of acceptance, Harriman shaped a new life, not because she felt better, but because her illness brought a shift in her perspective:

75

I try to contribute something meaningful to every day. I picture each day as a canvas, and my life as a palette of colors. I have learned to value the painting that emerges. I walk more slowly now, and stop to notice the tiny details that make up the whole of life: the child playing marbles on the porch, the dog waiting for his master to come out of the store. At home, my backyard garden is blossoming and growing and reminds me that life comes in many forms. I have learned that my life is different than it used to be, but it is still my life, and I am truly grateful for it.

When you're first diagnosed with a chronic illness, the last thing on your mind is creating a fulfilling life. Mere survival becomes your primary goal. For an initial "shock phase," you're so caught up in the task of simply managing your emotions and the changes in your body and lifestyle, actually *living* seems out of the question.

As time passes, you gain a level of acceptance, and you realize, like Patricia Harriman, that you can go about living again. Life will be different, in some ways better, in some ways worse, but the bottom line is, *it is a life.* You still have gifts and talents, spring continues to bless the earth each year, and the special people who selflessly love you still knock at your door.

It's time to reenter the world, to do the things you used to do, whether its going to the park with your kids, hanging out with your friends—or resuming your career.

In the following pages, we'll talk about returning to work after an absence due to chronic illness—and what happens when you can't go back.

RETURNING TO WORK: THE EMOTIONS
Strap in for Another Turbulent Ride

For those of you ready to dive back into your career, facing the workaday life can be at once joyous and

DON'T QUIT!

I have a few words of advice for those recently diagnosed: *Don't quit your job!* (That is, unless your physician advises you to do so.) I have met many people in the beginning stages of illness who are dealing with so much physical pain, raw emotion, medical tests, and doctor appointments that they say, "To heck with it, I can't even think about work."

Look into all your options before taking this drastic measure. Talk with your employer about what's going on. Talk to your physician. See if you can take an extended leave, adjust your hours, or switch to more manageable responsibilities. Know your legal rights under the Family Medical Leave Act (FMLA), which offers unpaid leave and other protections in many cases. Many employers have even more liberal policies than provided by law, so investigate your employer's policies.

If you quit your job, you may be adding more stress in your life than you intended to take away. You may be jeopardizing your insurance, and you will be eliminating a future source of income when your health improves. If you own your own business, have a discussion with your physician about how your illness is likely to affect your productivity, become familiar with your disability coverage, and work your illness into your business plans.

frightening. On one hand, you may feel elation that you are well enough to *get out.* On the other, you are entering uncharted territory: How will I juggle my doctor appointments with my work schedule? What if I can't handle my job? How will my coworkers react to me?

It's important to realize that this emotional pinball round is completely natural, and soon you'll regain your footing and fall into a new pattern of "normal."

Relief and Inspiration: Yes! I Can Work!

One of the hidden benefits of living with a chronic illness is that we get to appreciate, I mean *really* appreciate what we have. I will never say, "I wish I didn't have to work," because I know how very blessed I am that I *can* work. I have experienced severe pain and symptoms that have kept me bedridden for weeks. During this time, every good day was precious. After one good day strung into the next, and I gained enough stamina to head back to work, the feeling I had was pure gratitude.

Many of us find inspiration in our diseases as we return to the workplace. Audrey Kron, author of *Meeting the Challenge: Living with Chronic Illness,* writes, "Having Crohn's disease was an important part of why I became a psychotherapist. I went back to school so that I could work with people struggling with chronic illness. I have heard of others who became doctors, nurses, nutritionists, or sales representatives for drug companies."[1]

Joan Friedlander says her battle with Crohn's disease led her to shed a low-paying job and begin her practice as a career coach. "I was accepting employment situations that did not provide financial sufficiency and that were dead-ends in terms of fulfilling my desire to more directly make a difference in the lives of others. I decided enough was enough. I declared I would find a job that would pay me what I was worth—one of the lessons I learned because of my illness. It takes a bit of a leap of faith to imagine that you can use illness and disease to inform you about what is not working for you in your life."[2]

Work is the true elixir of life. The busiest man is the happiest man.

—Sir Theodore Martin

Self-Doubt: What If I Don't Make It?

Positives are always tempered with negatives, and so it is when you return to work. Though you may feel relieved that you can work, you are likely riddled with self-doubt. "What will my career look like now that I can't be at the office fifty hours a week?" "Will I advance?" "How will others perceive me?" Here's some advice that will help you take the punch out of that nagging self-deprecation.

Don't Expect to Go in at 100 Percent—You'll end up beating yourself up if you set unrealistic expectations. I know it's hard to think otherwise, since the only marker you have is your performance prior to becoming ill, but please try. Take it slow. Do less than you think you can in the beginning, and incrementally ramp up to a level where you feel comfortable. Don't worry about the implications this will have on your career. Right now, it's more important for you to discover how much you are able to work so you can properly gauge your capabilities in the future.

Set Your Own Limits—Communicate with your coworkers if you feel pressured to work to a level you aren't ready to handle. By setting realistic limits, you won't disappoint yourself or your colleagues.

Realize Your Strengths and Weaknesses—Work within your limits. If you have to stand several hours at a time on the job, for instance, and you are concerned you won't be able to anymore, talk to your employer to make adjustments. Play to your strengths, too. Let's say you are a lawyer. Your background is in litigation, but you know you are a skilled researcher. You are concerned that your body won't meet the physical demands of litigation: traveling, being on your feet for long stretches, strenuous interviews. Request that you be used as a researcher instead—a job where you can sit down and use your brain, instead of your body.

Remember, Your Health Is Priority One—The truth is, you may not be able to successfully resume your career. What's important is that you try. But don't push yourself at the expense of your health. Don't block that

BEWARE OF OVERCOMPENSATION!

Earlier in my career, I would give 150 percent to my employer. I often felt desperate: I couldn't afford to lose a job because of health insurance. I felt I was in more jeopardy of getting the ax than the average person because of my health issues. If I proved myself when I was well, I reasoned, then when I had to take work off, my employer would be less likely to get rid of me.

The result: I overcompensated. I did way more than was necessary to get the job done. I put in lots of overtime and ran myself ragged. I simply didn't have a full sense of who I was, and that giving 100 percent was enough. I have since come to understand my tendency to overdo it, and can now counter the negative self-talk with truthful reminders. Giving a solid day's work is sufficient. If it's not, the issue is with my employer and not me.

voice in your head that says, "I'm tired" or, "That hurts." Above all, shut out the voice that says, "If you weren't such a weakling, you could finish this project." Such internal rumblings make you push past your breaking point, like you used to. The rules have changed, and you can't do that anymore. There is too much at stake— your health and your career.

Communicate When You Need Help—Like most people, I get in over my head. It is not easy for me to say "no" because I get so enthusiastic about projects. As a result, I've found myself drowning. If you get into this situation, don't wait until the last minute to let someone know.

Give the project back or ask for help, so your employer will have enough time to find the necessary resources to get the job done.

Envy: Why Is Everyone Else So Lucky?

When you hang out at the water cooler and discuss the weekend, you will hear stories of ski trips and late-night parties. I used to feel like an old curmudgeon when I'd hear about my coworkers antics. Oh, to be healthy and free so I can run with the wind or ski down mountains!

It's not easy to temper such pangs of jealousy. The truth is my coworkers do get to frolic in their off time, while I'm at home recuperating from the work week.

To envy I say, "Don't waste your time!" When you compare yourself to others, you are buying into the Damaged Goods Syndrome. This practice is one of the single most destructive things you can do to your self-esteem, and for what? What is it buying you? Nothing but longing for a life that you don't know anything about and potentially isn't that great after all. Plenty of "healthy" people are miserable. *Internal health* leads to happiness. The beauty of this truth is you will always have the ability to create a healthy inner you, no matter how ill your body becomes.

Worry: What Will They Think?

Whether they admit it or not, everyone worries about what other people think, especially when it comes to work. How can we avoid it when so much of our career success is based on the opinions of others: our employers, our key clients, and sometimes even our coworkers. The worry compounds when we have to ask for time off to manage our health.

One way to avoid the worry is to keep your private life private. Your coworkers don't need to know where you are going in the middle of the afternoon—for all they know you could have an important meeting with a client. As long as you are open with your direct superi-

WAIT TO WORRY

Before you let worrying about a problem about work stunt you, see if there is something you can do to solve it.

The Worry: Too Much to Do
   Make a To-Do List—Seeing it on paper will help you plan your time.
   Get Organized—Buy a Palm Pilot, Day-Timer, or other personal assistant tool. Fretting about missing appointments is a total waste of time.
   Don't Procrastinate—Procrastination leads to worry. Just get the task done, so you can cross it off your list and move on to the next item.
   Pare Down—You may have too much going on. Look at your life and see where you can simplify. Ask your employer to lighten your workload.

The Worry: Coworker Conflict
   Go to the Source—Nothing is more stressful than personality conflicts at work. Such a problem can make it

or about your whereabouts, keep everyone else in suspense. You don't need to explain yourself.

Another way to temper anxiety is to remind yourself of this important message: "It is none of your business what other people think." You can't control other people's opinions, but you can control yours. Stop thinking of yourself as Damaged Goods and start thinking of yourself as a viable asset to the workplace. If you *know* you are doing the best you can do, then who the heck cares what other people think? The naysayers will even-

difficult to get your job done. I've found the very best way to solve these kinds of issues is to go to the source. Don't complain to your friends, go to the person you are having difficulties with, and hash it out with him or her.

The Worry: General Anxiety

Talk to a Good Friend—Even if you don't know what's upsetting you, a good friend or counselor can have just the magic words to make you realize the source of your anxiety. A new perspective might offer new solutions.

Check in with Your Body—Are you taking care of yourself? Are you exercising and eating a balanced diet? How are your meds? Do they need adjustment? Could they be causing emotional strain?

The Worry: Job Dissatisfaction

Talk to the Problem Solver—So often we go to every Tom, Dick, and Harry with our woes, when it's really Susan who has the problem-solving power. If you are unhappy with a situation at work, go straight to the person who can make a meaningful change.

tually wake up and see, despite your unorthodox work schedule, you are a hard-working employee.

Also helpful is to investigate the source of your worry so you can root out the problem. I call this strategy "Wait to Worry" (see above). When you begin to fret, stop. First ask yourself, "What's truly bothering me?" Then before you let yourself dive into a paralyzing panic session see if there are simple things you can do to alleviate the stress.

Avoidance: I Don't Want to Go!

There will be mornings that you will want to hide under the covers. This is normal. Remember, even physically healthy people feel this way. When I have mornings like this, I employ the magic of "Acting as If." Once I get to work, I usually feel better. I also remind myself that after I get my brain moving in a work direction, it will stop focusing in the pain direction, which is always better for my psyche.

But take heed: Be sure to check in with your body. If you want to stay under the covers because your body is displaying some new symptom or pain, take yourself to the doctor instead of work.

Feeling Trapped: I'll Never Be Able to Leave My Job!

What if you are returning to a job that you don't like? You need the money, and you need the insurance. You think, "Who's going to hire me now that I have an illness? I better stick with what I have."

I understand this feeling. It's an issue I've had to cope with my entire career. But if I listened to the voice in my head that said I couldn't leave a job because of my condition, I wouldn't be writing this book today. For starters, lots of people will hire you despite your chronic illness. Under the Americans with Disabilities Act (ADA), it's discriminatory for an employer not to hire you because of a health condition. I don't want to sound naive—certainly there is discrimination in the world—but don't let fear of discrimination stop you from trying.

In terms of insurance: Despite recent reforms that I'll get into later, health insurance can certainly make chronically ill people feel trapped in their jobs, mainly because most U.S. citizens—64.1 percent in the year 2000, to be exact—are covered through an employer.[3]

While a physically healthy person might be willing to take the risk and go without insurance as she job hunts or tries to contract, a chronically ill person simply does not have that option. Getting individual insurance to fill the gap isn't always viable because the premiums can be outrageous, especially for patients with—I like to say—a *colorful* medical history.

I understand why you'd want to throw up your hands and say, "It's not worth it! I'm never leaving my job!" Though the temptation may be great, I urge you to instead zero in on getting "unstuck."

Devise a Plan—You may have to return to a job you don't like to buy some time while you figure out what's next. Just giving yourself breathing room to dream a little will make you feel less trapped.

Focus on What You Are Gaining—Remember that every job, even if you don't like it, is giving you valuable work skills.

Get the Facts—Research your insurance situation. Sometimes what you imagine is worse than what is. Can you buy your own insurance for a couple of months? How much will COBRA coverage cost, and how long will it protect you? Can you switch to your spouse's insurance? Once you get answers, you can make better decisions about your future.

Dabble—Take a class or join a club in the career area that interests you. See if you really like it before taking the plunge. Dabbling will help you make strides toward your goal and build your resume at the same time. It also ensures you aren't falling victim to the ol' "grass-is-greener" syndrome.

RETURNING TO WORK: THE FACTS

Learn Your Workplace Rights

As you mesh your work life with your new life, get ready to face unfamiliar realities, such as working half-

85

FOR LOVE OR HEALTH INSURANCE?

NOTE: A few years back I wrote a humorous piece for a kidney disease newsletter that poked fun at the insurance issue—this was before the passage of legislative reforms, when the situation was even more dire than it is today. Here is a pared down version of it, just for laughs.

So often you hear romantics bemoan, "Oh, what we do for love!" Their list of antics may include buying an expensive box of chocolates, wooing their love over a candlelight dinner, or tossing a dangerously flirtatious glance across the room.

People living with chronic illness have a similar phrase, "What we do for health insurance." But the things we do aren't nearly as cute. Instead, our tactics look something like this: Forget about the sweet guy I madly love; he doesn't have health coverage. I'm more interested in the grumpy old guy over there leaning on his Mercedes. Surely I can get on his policy!

Yes, we do crazy things for health insurance. We stay in miserable relationships and miserable jobs rather than giving up our "benefits." We get on long waiting lists for high-risk plans, and we're thrilled when we're accepted, even though we're paying obnoxious premiums.

One day a friend of mine faxed me an ad. It read, "Your Preexisting Condition Just Became Medical History." A glimmer of hope! Surely we're on to something, I thought. I dialed the number and quickly realized getting through their phone system was part of their pre-qualifying test. First they judged my mental competency

time because that's all your body can handle, requesting special accommodations or dealing with coworkers' lack of understanding. You'll also hear yourself asking questions you never thought would come out of your mouth like, "If I alter my work schedule to fit in my doctor visits, can my boss demote me?" This new territory

by asking me to navigate an amazingly complicated phone tree. I failed. I finally pushed the right number after five repeats of the menu.

They then examined my physical stamina by leaving me on hold for what seemed an eternity. Finally, a very nice lady answered and asked how she could help me.

"I would like to know if you would insure me," I said. "I had a kidney transplant and have no sign of complications."

Without skipping a beat, she said, "Oh, no, we don't take your disease."

"Well, what is this preexisting ad all about?" I shot back.

"There are a few preexisting conditions we are accepting, just not yours," she replied.

I asked to see the list. I wanted to find out if hang nails or split ends were on it. I thanked her and hung up.

Today, I am fortunate enough to have a health insurance plan through my husband's work. (And no, I didn't marry him just for his insurance, but it was a nice fringe benefit.) Still, I went without insurance for a while, and I know how frightening it can be. I hope our government addresses these issues and comes through with a solid plan for all people to have access to affordable healthcare.

For myself, I'd like to go back to the old days when a night out with my friends meant discussing what we do for love, instead of what we do for health insurance!

is unwelcome, often uncomfortable, and confusing to manage for everyone with a chronic illness—the seasoned vets and the just-diagnosed alike. For starters, you need to be aware of the ADA. While specific questions should be addressed to an appropriate public or private counselor or attorney, some background facts about the ADA as it currently exists are important to know.

The Basics of the ADA

Under the ADA, employers cannot discriminate against people with disabilities and are required to make reasonable accommodations so the disabled can continue working. I suggest reading the ADA. A copy of this landmark legislation is available on the Internet at the United States Department of Justice's Web site at www.usdoj.gov or at your local Social Security office. It's also wise to read your employee handbook to see what your company's policies are beyond the ADA. In the meantime, here's an overview of the legislation:

What Is 'Disabled'?—A disability is a physical or mental impairment that substantially limits one or more of your major life activities.[4] Such activities include "seeing, hearing, speaking, walking, breathing, performing manual tasks, learning, caring for oneself, and working." For instance, people with conditions like epilepsy, paralysis, AIDS, and individuals with substantial hearing or visual impairment are covered.[5]

What Is 'Discrimination'?—Discrimination means your employer is denying you equal jobs or benefits, is limiting your opportunities or status, or is not making reasonable accommodations because of your disability. A prospective employer is discriminating against you if he won't hire you because you are disabled. Under the ADA, your spouse or relatives can't be discriminated against because of your disability, and if anyone harasses you or retaliates against you for filing charges of discrimination, that's illegal.[6]

What Is 'Reasonable Accommodation'?—Employers with fifteen or more employees[7] need to make the facilities their employees use accessible to people with disabilities. You can request that your employer restructure your job, modify your work schedule, or move you to a vacant position to accommodate your illness.[8] If making such accommodations leads to "undue hardship"—in other words, it would seriously harm your employer or alter the nature of the business—he may be exempt. Hardship is reviewed on a case-by-case basis.[9]

So how does all of this apply to chronic illness? Let me show you through a real-life example about a blind woman in Baltimore. She applied for a teaching position at an elementary school, and, according to the woman, a representative at the Baltimore City Public School System offered her a teaching position after two interviews during which she had used a cane. After she mentioned that she would soon be picking up her new service animal, she said, the school's principal withdrew the offer rather than allow her to bring a dog in the building; the woman filed a complaint under the ADA through local channels, and the Department of Justice later filed a lawsuit. The court agreed the woman had been mistreated, and under the agreed consent decree, the school system will pay her $55,000, ensure that all personnel are trained in ADA law, and designate an employee to serve as the ADA coordinator.[10]

If you suspect your rights are being violated, you can file a claim. If you're thinking about filing a claim, be sure you document *everything.* Keep a detailed record of instances of discrimination, including all the parties who were involved, witnesses, dates, and times. The more hard information you have, the easier the process will be. Consult an attorney if you think you might have a claim, since certain time requirements may apply. When it comes to legal claims, delay can be disaster.

Finding ADA Resources

The ADA can be confusing, and hiring an attorney can be costly. If you need guidance, these groups can help.

Patient Advocate Foundation—This nonprofit organization offers a wealth of information on the ADA, and the FMLA, and also assists people in protecting their health insurance. The group puts out several useful brochures, including one that details both the ADA and the FMLA. You can read "First My Illness, Now Job Discrimination: Steps To Resolution," on-line at www.patientadvocate.org, or you can order a free copy by dialing 800-532-5274.

Independent Living Centers—Known as the Center for Independent Living, this organization helps people with disabilities live on their own through skills workshops, employment and housing services, legal advocacy, and other support programs. There are hundreds of these centers throughout the country. Look up your local office in the phone book or on-line for contact information.

Disability and Business Technical Assistance Centers—The purpose of these centers is to educate and train people on the ADA. They have a toll-free hotline at 800-949-4232.

Equal Employment Opportunity Commission—This is a good place to gather basic facts about the ADA. You can find the Web site at www.eeoc.gov or call 800-669-4000.

Pick Your Battles

Life is either a daring adventure or nothing.

—Helen Keller

It's one thing to know your rights; it's another to exercise them. Pick your battles. Try out creative solutions to problems before throwing down the ADA card. If your employer is trying her best, by all means, work with her.

To understand what I'm saying, listen to this story. Remember Bryon Vouga, my friend with renal failure who biked across country? Not too long ago he approached me with a problem. Vouga was being dialyzed three times a week for four hours at a time. As a teacher, he was able to leave school after his last class and get to the dialysis unit in time for the final appointment. There he would grade papers and plan his lessons. Everything was going like clockwork until the dialysis unit changed its hours, and the administrator told him he'd have to show up earlier. When Vouga explained that he couldn't leave school, she suggested he ask for "reasonable accommodation."

He said to me, "Yeah, sure, I can ask for 'reasonable accommodation,' and the school will have to comply, but the reality is, I may not continue to advance in my career. If I leave early three times a week, that would not be a good thing."

I hate to say it, but I agreed with him. Regardless of what his school would actually do, I didn't think Vouga should take such a chance at this young stage in his career.

I suggested he find another dialysis unit—one that would offer treatment schedules before and after work hours. Shortly thereafter Vouga received a transplant, so he never had to face the dilemma. Had he asked for "reasonable accommodation" he would have benefited in the short-term, but, in the long-term, I wonder if he would have lost out.

The Basics of the FMLA

The FMLA is important to know about when you need to take large chunks of time off, or if you need to cut back your hourly or weekly schedule.

It entitles eligible employees to take twelve weeks of unpaid, job-protected leave per year for family and medical reasons.[11] The FMLA applies to employers and public agencies that employ fifty or more employees. To be eligible for the FMLA under the current law, you must have worked for a U.S.-based employer for a total of twelve months. During that time, you had to have worked at least 1,250 hours.[12]

FMLA Benefits

Leave—You are allowed off twelve unpaid workweeks during a one-year period for a variety of reasons, one of which is a serious health condition. You may schedule your leave intermittently—meaning you can take blocks of time off or adjust your daily or weekly hours to accommodate your situation.[13]

Health Insurance Protection—When you take leave under the FMLA, your employer is not allowed to stop your health benefits.[14]

Job Protection—When you return to work, you must be restored to your original or an equivalent job with the same pay and benefits.[15]

If it hasn't already, you can see how the FMLA might come in handy for you. If you need to take two months off for surgery, for instance, or if you are suddenly admitted to the hospital and you discover you won't be coming back to work for a month, you won't have to worry about suddenly getting the ax at work or losing your health benefits.

Issues at Work

Now that we've covered the ADA and FMLA, let's get into a few of the issues that may come up for you at work.

Should I Tell My Boss I Have an Illness?—According to the federal government, you don't have a duty to tell an employer about your condition unless it will impede your ability to perform your job.[16] I am not against disclosing your condition to a supervisor, but I suggest that you do it on a "need-to-know basis." Wait until you feel it's necessary to tell your boss—for instance, if you need to take time off. If you say too much too soon, your supervisor may prejudge the kind of work you are able to do, or may withhold projects, thinking she's doing you a favor. Let your employer judge you on your work alone, not a potential future bout you may have with illness.

Should I Tell My Coworkers I Have an Illness?—There are compelling arguments on both sides. Keeping your illness to yourself, if you can, tends to keep things simple. When employees disclose their health status to peers, a complex work environment can evolve, according to Norma Jean Vescovo, the executive director of the Independent Living Center of Southern California. "I have found employees who reveal their disability to coworkers tend to get more assistance than they need. These employees have to make sure to keep their position whole. They should not expect to be treated differently." Vescovo says the coworkers may overextend their help and then take credit for the work the ill person should have been doing. Such a dynamic will undermine the chronically ill person's position at work, which can be an unhealthy environment for everyone.

That said, more often than not, my coworkers have known about my kidney disease. This is partly because for me the line between coworker and friend is often quite blurry, and partly because circumstances—like needing to take a leave for surgery—often made it clear to everyone I had a unique health situation. I'm also an open person, and it is natural for me to tell people about myself. I think it helps people to relate to me better and sets them at ease. It's up to you to assess yourself, your office environment, and your relationships with coworkers to determine if disclosure is the best path for you.

In any case, I suggest you save the gory details about your appointments, symptoms, and how bad you feel for your support group. If you tell your coworkers too much, you run the risk of scaring them off, appearing

JUGGLING WORK AND MEDICAL APPOINTMENTS

Taking care of yourself with an illness can be, in itself, a full-time job. So how do you blend your work schedule with your medical schedule—and stay sane in the process?

Book Your Appointment at the End of the Day—That way, you don't have to return to work after the visit. This eases running around, and allows you to take less time off since you don't have to waste the minutes commuting back to the office.

Book Appointments Far in Advance—If your appointments are routine, book them as far ahead as possible to ensure you'll get the time slot you need.

Get to Know the Front Office People—Tell them about your tight schedule, and ask them to do their best to work around it. Remember, you are the customer.

Tie up Loose Ends before You Leave Work—If you are able, schedule appointments at the endpoint of projects, so you know things will be sewn up before you leave. If you aren't needed while you are gone, your absence will be less remarked upon.

Communicate—Don't be ashamed to leave the office for a couple of hours. You have the *right* to take care of your health. If you act sorry or sneak out of work, it will most likely make other people think you *are* doing something sneaky, such as interviewing for another job. If you are up-front, and don't make excuses on your way out the door, your coworkers will be more likely to accept your early departures.

like a whiner, or having them judge you based on your illness versus your performance at work.

What If My Job Duties become Too Strenuous?—If you can no longer work in your field, speak to your boss or human resources manager about transferring to a less strenuous job or adjusting your schedule. Be open to creative solutions. One option gaining ground in many companies is job sharing, where two people share the duties of one full-time job. They work out the details of the schedule themselves. This is a great idea for people who are on dialysis three times a week or balance a heavy treatment schedule.

If your employer doesn't have an alternative schedule or position for you, talk to the EEOC, a social worker, or someone knowledgeable about the ADA, and ask them to advise you about your best course of action. Whatever you do, don't quit. You can use the law to insist that your current employer accommodate you. However, if you quit voluntarily, it can be much more difficult to force a previous employer to hire you back and come into compliance with the law.

Coping with Coworkers' Prejudice

As people find out about your illness, either through word of mouth or because it is visibly apparent, their reactions will vary widely. Some will act naturally. Some will be overly sympathetic. Some will avoid you. And some will lash out with discriminatory behavior. I *wish* I could say you will never encounter prejudice, but I'd be lying.

Discrimination can be as simple as being excluded from the office social life or as overt as being rejected for a promotion because you look or sound different. Rhonda Brooks, who has lived with renal disease for twelve years, believes prejudice kept her from getting a job as a controller. She tells about the time she was passed up for the position:

> I was in the final stages of the interview process. This was the last interview before they made a hiring decision. It was down to me and another person. One of the VPs noticed I had a gap in work history and was curious how I

supported myself. I replied, 'I attended college for four years.' I was trying to get around the question. He was insistent, and I told him, 'I left my previous job and took long-term disability because I had kidney problems. I ended up on dialysis and now I have a successful transplant. I can do the job and have no health difficulties. I even completed my degree while on dialysis.' In an instant, his attitude changed from positive and happy to stunned silence. Up until that point, I was the top candidate. Needless to say, I didn't get the job.

I believe prejudice is rooted in a lack of understanding. How you cope with it depends on what type of person you are and what kind of discrimination you are experiencing.

In terms of the more subtle forms of bias, such as exclusion and gossip, I've found the best approach is to befriend my coworkers. This helps in two ways. One, it lets them know me, which educates them about my condition. The more they understand me, the less likely they are to draw prejudicial conclusions. The other benefit of becoming pals with coworkers is, when I sense tension, it's easier for me to open a discussion and find out what's really going on. By communicating directly, I nip any behind-my-face chatter in the bud.

When you are met with more extreme forms of discrimination, things get more complicated. My main advice is don't ignore it. If you are being bothered at work, talk to your supervisor, human resources manager, or seek counsel from one of the many organizations designed to aid people in such situations.

Discrimination is extremely difficult to look in the face. When it happens to you, I know it can be devastating. The key here is to point it out, and don't let it knock you down permanently. For every ignorant person who spreads hate, ignorance, or stereotypes,

OF COURSE I'VE BEEN TO SURGERY

When I was working as a sales manager for a catheter company, one of my jobs was to serve as backup for the sales reps, who would accompany doctors into surgery to instruct them on proper placement of the product. Prior to surgery I was waiting in the doctor's lounge chatting with some of the nurses who knew my background. They asked me about my transplant.

The doctor overheard this conversation but didn't say anything. Later, during surgery, he asked in disbelief, "So, you're a transplant patient?"

"Yes," I said.

"And you're a manager?"

"Yes," I said. Clearly he was struggling with the idea that I could be a transplant patient and handle a demanding position.

"Really? How did you get this job?" he asked.

"In the interview, they asked me if I'd ever been to surgery," I explained. "I answered, 'Thirty-four times.' They just didn't ask me if I was awake."

there are many others who will see and appreciate you as you are.

ABCs of Insurance

I include insurance in this chapter on work because so many Americans are insured through their jobs. The two are often inexorably linked. We've already discussed how the insurance burden may make you feel "trapped" in your position. Now let's dig a little deeper.

There are several types of insurance for which you can apply; the most common is group coverage, provided through an employer. You may also opt for individual, but the premiums can be extremely high. Social

Security Disability Insurance, which encompasses Medicare and Medicaid, is reserved primarily for the elderly, disabled, low-income, and unemployed. In a pinch, there is also COBRA. Current COBRA requires employers to let you continue group coverage for typically eighteen months after you've left your job. While COBRA helps temporarily, it's a short-term fix, and the monthly premiums can be exorbitant.

Judging by this quick synopsis, our insurance options are limited—especially when compared to Britain or Canada's federally sponsored programs—but at least we *have* options. Prior to 1996, when congress enacted the Health Insurance Portability and Accountability Act (HIPAA), people with chronic illness could get denied health benefits all-too-easily.[17]

HIPAA limits an insurer's ability to deny you coverage due to "preexisting conditions,"[18] and makes it illegal for group health plans to discriminate based on your or your family members' medical histories. Before the HIPAA, if your employer changed carriers, or if you switched jobs and signed up for new health insurance, the new insurer could refuse to accept you.[19]

While the law is an improvement, there are still concerns, according to a March 2000 report by the Syracuse University's Center for Policy Research. The researchers found that "despite the HIPAA, serious or chronic illness might continue to adversely affect the adequacy of coverage, and additional health insurance reform may be warranted."[20]

Chronically ill patients still have to deal with caps on lifetime payouts for certain illnesses. Further, the HIPAA does not limit the amount you can be charged for the policy,[21] and "there is evidence that the insurers are responding to HIPAA with higher cost health insurance and even avoiding statutory requirements in some cases."[22]

DOS AND DON'TS TO PROTECT YOUR COVERAGE

The Centers for Medicare and Medicaid Services, available at www.hcfa.gov, suggests taking the following precautions when changing your job or insurance provider.

Do Ask for a Certificate of Creditable Coverage—Such a certificate shows how long you have had health coverage. This can be important when you enroll in a new group health plan or get individual coverage.

Do Consider Accepting Continuation Coverage—If COBRA, Temporary Continuation of Coverage, or State Continuation Coverage is available and offered to you, you should seriously consider accepting it. If you do not accept and exhaust the coverage, you may lose some of your HIPAA rights and protections.

Don't Allow a Break in Coverage—If you wait sixty-three or more full days in a row to get health coverage, you will not get credit for your previous coverage, and you might lose some of your HIPAA rights and protections.

Do Be Cautious When Converting Coverage—Some insurance issuers offer the chance to convert from a group health plan to an individual policy. This means that you would still have a policy with the same issuer, but it would be an individual policy. The benefits may not be the same, and generally the premiums would be more expensive. It is important to remember that if you accept a conversion policy, you may not be HIPAA-eligible for individual coverage after the conversion policy ends.

Do Shop Around—Different people will have different options when losing or changing health coverage. Be sure you research your options and know your rights.

That said, the law does prevent employee-sponsored insurers from charging one individual a higher premium based on that individual's health status. For example, if you have diabetes, you cannot be charged a higher premium because of that medical condition. An individual must be charged the same premium as "similarly situated individuals." Similarly situated individuals are, for example, other people in the same employee category or geographic location as you.[23]

When Something Goes Wrong

What can you do when you feel you've been unjustly treated by an insurance carrier? If you pay all or part of your premium, call the insurance company directly. Ask for your claim to be reviewed and a report sent back to you. If your company pays your premium, contact your supervisor or employee benefits administrator. From what I have heard, many companies are afraid to rock the boat with their health insurance carriers for fear of their rates being raised. Don't despair and be persistent! Keep copies of all claims and document all your conversations, including the date, time, name, and phone number of the person you contacted. If the review doesn't go your way, contact your State Insurance Commission for help. Still no action? Seek legal counsel promptly to avoid missing any deadlines. In general, you should become aware of applicable legal deadlines before you start.

HIRE ME!
Job Hunting with a Chronic Illness

Looking for a job can be brutal. It wears away at everyone's self esteem, but can be especially difficult for people who already have a touch of the Damaged Goods Syndrome. When you start feeling "less than" during your job search, remember the words of Malia Langden, a young woman wise beyond her years.

Langden had kidney failure in her teens and, since then, she has had to regularly dialyze and has had several surgeries. Despite these barriers, in May 2001, she graduated with a master's degree in fine arts. When we last spoke, she was at an impasse. Like many recent graduates, she had no clue what she wanted to do next. But she wasn't letting that get her down. "Dealing with serious health issues at an early age has helped me to gain perspective," she explained. "When my peers were stressing out over grades or what college they would get into, I was simply thankful that my health was well. This is something of which I constantly have to remind myself. When I am discouraged over career issues, insignificant or material things, I must remember to be thankful that I have the energy and good health to be able to pursue these things in the first place."

Researching a New Field and Getting Connected

If you are switching careers, I suggest you do some deep research on the field before sending out a single resume. Because of our dependence on health benefits and our special requirements in the workplace, changing jobs is a few degrees riskier for us than the average person. It is important that you make sure you are committed to your new endeavor before you quit what you have.

The following suggestions will help you get the information you need. Most are also great ways to make contacts and gain skills if you are reentering the job market after a long absence.

Attend Conferences and Seminars—Conferences are great because they show you a microcosm of your field of interest. In one weekend you can learn just about everything you need to know. What are the people like? What's the industry culture like? What are the big issues? They are also excellent for contacts and to prepare you for an upcoming interview.

Enroll in a Local College Class—A high-level class is an excellent way to see if you are interested in a new field. Whether you realize it or not, classes give you practical experience. If you participated in a group research project in your Social Behavior of Dolphins class, for example, you can talk about the results in your upcoming interview with the Maritime Lab. I suggest you get to know your professor, who could be a contact or reference when you are ready to begin interviewing.

Interview—Accept every opportunity to interview, even if you don't think you want the job. You can tell a lot about a company—the culture, the people, the type of work you will perform—when you interview. An interview can be a firsthand education on both the company, and the field as a whole. The other benefit: The more interviews you go on, the better you'll get. Since living with a chronic illness often damages your confidence, it's very important to practice, practice, practice.

Internships—If you have the time and the ability to work for little or no pay, do an internship. You'll get on-the-job training without a long-term commitment. You'll be able to see if this is the kind of work you could do for the next few years. Not to mention the fact that internships often lead to jobs.

Volunteer—Like an internship, volunteering is a hands-on way to discover whether you'll like a new field. It's also a great way to build the connections you'll need if you are switching fields or are reentering the workplace.

At one point in my career, I was working at Disney, when all I really wanted was to work in the renal care industry and help other patients. That's when I decided that if I didn't have enough experience to get paid, perhaps I could offer my enthusiasm for free to get the experience I needed. I joined renal patient services committees and started meeting people.

Ultimately I earned a seat on the Patient Advisory Committee for the Southern California Renal Disease Council. The council sent me to a meeting in Florida as its representative. Impressed by my passion for the cause, the owner of a renal care company offered me a job on the spot. That was my start working in the field I love. If you're long on enthusiasm and short on resume, volunteering is the way to go.

The Interview Balancing Act: What to Reveal or Conceal

You have a hot lead on the dream job; now if you could just get past the interview. Interviewing is hard for everybody, but it's especially difficult for people with chronic illness. For one, you may have visible signs of your condition. Also, sticky questions can surface

about whether you are capable. Following are some tips to help you paddle through the murky waters.

Know How Much You Should Say about Your Illness—There are legal protections in place so you won't be discrimi-

LORI'S TOOLBOX

eight

LORI'S *HOW TO WOW* GUIDEBOOK:
Use These Chronically Happy Tips for the Interview

The ol' Damaged Goods mentality tends to resurface when we put ourselves on the line, and we are never more on the line than when we interview for a job, especially if it's a position we *really* want. Don't despair! Dig into your Toolbox and find your *How to Wow* guidebook (below), and the job will be yours! As you go through this exercise, fight the temptation to listen to the negative voice that says you are a less desirable candidate because of your illness. You are as skilled as the next guy; all you have to do is prepare, prepare, prepare, and your interviewer will see your value, too.

Write out Questions and Answers—If you are able to anticipate your interviewer's questions, you'll avoid being caught off guard, which makes all of us stumble. I'm not suggesting "canned" answers. I am suggesting that you carefully think through *and write down* what you'll say to

nated against as you interview. Be aware that a potential employer is not allowed to ask you about your disability. She can ask, however, about your ability to perform job functions. Also, she can condition her job offer on the result of a job-related medical exam, but only if the same test is required for all entering employees in the same job category.[24]

Be Ready for Questions about Gaps in Your Employment— To fill in those untidy gaps on your resume, you may want to discuss volunteer service and/or schooling, especially if it relates to the job for which you are applying. For instance, let's say you had to stop working because you needed a series of operations. During your recovery time between procedures, you volun-

the basics: "Where do you see yourself in five years?", "What are your career goals?", and "What is your greatest weakness?"

Watch Yourself—Videotape yourself and have a loved one critique you—with brutal honesty.

Learn Speaking Techniques—I joined Toastmasters to improve my public speaking ability, but the skills I learned there also greatly helped me with my interviewing skills. Toastmasters or a public speaking class could be useful for you, too, especially if you have a fear of interviewing or speaking in front of groups of people.

Do Mock Interviews—Work on presenting yourself with poise and confidence. And once again, know your rights by reading up on the ADA. Avoid walking into an interview with a shamed look that pleads, "Please hire me. I'm sick, and I really need the money!" You may have an illness, but you haven't lost your ability to work hard and to be responsible, resourceful, and creative. It's all still there! What more could an employer want?

teered for a nonprofit group and gave speeches to youth groups. You could tell the interviewer something like, "After I left my job at ABC Company in 1994, I volunteered at XYZ Help the Kids. There, I honed my speaking skills, which would be an asset to your company." That way, you will truthfully account for gaps in your employment while promoting your candidacy for the job—without disclosing more information than the interviewer is entitled to know.

Don't Try to Hide Your Disability—If your disability is noticeable, the best solution is to disarm people by being honest and confident about it. Don't try to hide it, address it, if it seems appropriate. If I am out to lunch with a prospective client, for instance, my knees creek when I get up from the table. I don't make a big deal about it, but I do say, "Excuse me, I am a little stiff today." I acknowledge my disability, but also make the other person feel at ease by showing them I am able to manage it.

How you respond to the comments and looks during the interview makes all the difference. If you have shame about your illness, it will project and make people feel uncomfortable. Conversely, if you are proud of who you are, your confidence will shine through. Like magic!

Take Steps Now to Avoid Problems in the Future

Whether drastic or simple, I suggest you take the initiative to make job-related changes on your terms, rather than waiting until, God forbid, your illness takes over and you are left without choices.

Taking charge means sitting down and looking at the long-term impact of your chronic illness. How much longer will you be able to work? Do you foresee changes in your body that will hinder your ability to do your present job? What can you do to protect yourself should these changes surface?

I don't believe that making a backup plan constitutes negative thinking, nor do I view such forethought as a pessimistic approach to living with a chronic illness. In fact, I think everyone, regardless of health, should have a Plan B. It just makes good sense.

Anthony Tusler, who has lived with a spinal cord injury since he was five years old, knows about planning for the future. Although he works as a technology consultant in the disability field, Tusler knows from literature that people with spinal cord injuries tend to lose much of their stamina as they age. Tusler also fears that the tendonitis in his shoulder, which he's developed from pushing his wheelchair, may get worse. As a result, Tusler has purchased an electric wheelchair and makes sure to reserve one whenever he travels to conferences. "I always have to plan ahead whenever I go to a new place. I can't assume that I can get to the same places as everyone else," he explains. "I need to always be looking for the accessible entrance, the curb cut, and easy-to-open door. When I am traveling on business or pleasure, planning ahead and being willing to change my plans is essential." Tusler also carefully balances his workload, so he doesn't take on too much, and he's prepared to use his social security disability pensions when working becomes too much.

In my case, as I've mentioned before, my knees are not as strong as I wish they were. Sometimes they cause me pain and prevent me from walking or standing as long as I'd like. Given the fact that living with a transplanted kidney means I will continue taking steroids and immunosuppressant drugs for the rest of my life (or the life of the organ), there is a good chance that my knee joints will always be problematic.

I must face the fact that there might come a time when I won't be able to get out and travel for business the way I do today. Therefore, I am learning as much about the computer as I possibly can so I can continue to be productive and support myself from home. On a more emotional level, I am preparing myself for that one day when I may need to sit rather than stand while giving an hour-long speech.

What's your Plan B?

GIVING UP YOUR CAREER

When Work Isn't an Option

Meaningful work helps meet that need we all have to make a difference, however big or small. Sick or healthy, we all need to be needed. For many, especially those who are single or without children, having a satisfying career helps scratch that itch for significance. Also, having a job often provides a much-needed diversion from the daily grind of living with ongoing medical concerns.

But what if that thing that gives you an alternate focus is taken away from you? Greg Falconer was faced with just this situation. After being diagnosed with kidney failure at age twenty-two, Falconer was forced to leave a job he enjoyed as an assistant parts manager at a car dealership.

"It was apparent that I could not go back to work. Some of it was physical, and there were obstacles related to obtaining health insurance. The fact is they didn't want to insure me," he explains.

Falconer says at first he worried about not contributing financially and that he would be unhappy without a professional outlet. "I'm the type of person who's always doing something. I'm not very sedentary. I grew up in a time when guys ask you what you do. And what they're asking is, 'Where do you work?' "

Falconer found a solution when his wife had a baby, Carolyn. "I became the stay-at-home dad, managing all the household chores," Falconer recalled. That was back in 1977. "Today, my wife and I adopted a little boy named Chance and have an opportunity at parenting all over again. ... Being a full-time dad is one of the most gratifying things I have ever done. People ask me if I work, and I say, 'Yes, I work everyday. I just don't get paid.' "

For Falconer, the end of his career didn't mean the end of the world. In fact, it meant the beginning of a new life, one that Falconer found just as fulfilling. Like Falconer, you can find things to do outside of your former career.

Look at your *List of Things You Can Do* (from the first Toolbox exercise) and, one by one, start doing them. You never know, you may tap into a whole new passion.

Results!
Why, man, I
have gotten
lots of results.
I know several
thousand
things that
won't work.

—Thomas
Edison

No Work Means No Money. What Am I Going to Do?

It's the classic one-two punch: First you get knocked down by a chronic illness, then, as you're flat on your back, you have to give up your job. Now you don't have insurance, but you still need medical care. The bills are piling up and you don't have any way to pay them. Hopefully this scary scenario isn't one you'll have to face. If you do, however, there are resources. You just need to know where to look.

Patient Advocate Foundation—This is a great place to start. The nonprofit group puts out *The National Financial Resource Guidebook for Patients,* which breaks down the options available to patients who need financial relief for stresses like housing, food, transportation, childcare, and insurance deductibles. The resources are listed on a state-by-state basis, which makes it easy to track down help in your specific region. The guidebook is searchable on-line at www.patientadvocate.org, or you can call 800-532-5274 to order a paper copy. The foundation will send you your state's listings at no charge, or you can purchase the entire book.

Protection and Advocacy Systems—Also known as P and As, these federally mandated disability rights agencies are all over the country. You'll have to look in the government pages in your phone book to locate the one nearest you, or you can search on-line at www.protectionandadvocacy.com. P and A agencies provide legal representation and other advocacy services to people with disabilities. In addition to monitoring conditions in facilities that care for disabled people, P and As make sure individuals with disabilities get full access to educational programs, financial entitlements, healthcare, accessible housing, and employment opportunities.

State Rehabilitation Centers—Every state offers vocational rehabilitation services. You'll have to look in the phone book for your state's agency; each one is called something slightly different. The goal of such organizations is to help individuals with disabilities get and keep jobs. Although you are not able to work right now, hooking up with such a center may help you explore your options, and you may be surprised at the scope of its offerings. In addition to job search and placement help, most rehab places offer counseling and guidance, diagnosis and some treatment of physical and mental impairments, some transportation, on-the-job or personal assistance services, and referrals, so you can get help from other government entities.

Turning to the Social Security Administration

Another place to turn for help is the Social Security Administration. This federal government agency has two programs that pay benefits to people with disabilities: Social Security Disability Insurance (SSDI) and Supplemental Security Income (SSI). Both are reserved for people who are unable to work—though you may be able to make a little bit of money and still receive some benefits. The more money you make, the fewer benefits you receive. SSDI is for individuals who paid into Social Security via taxes before they stopped working. SSI pays benefits based on a financial need. Many people who are on SSI get food stamps and Medicaid, which helps pay doctor and hospital bills.[25]

I have been on SSDI and am grateful that it was there when I needed it. But there is a price to pay for receiving benefits. You have very *little* money—meaning you live month-to-month with the specter of "What if they cut me off?" hanging over your head.

Also, it can be difficult to qualify for SSDI. You have to prove you are too sick to do just about anything, and this isn't always easy.

Several chronic illnesses, like chronic fatigue syndrome, are not diagnosed based on a conclusive set of tests. Rather, diagnoses are made based on the opinion of your doctor, which won't always carry the weight needed to qualify for social security. Applicants may need to see several doctors and submit multiple appeals before being accepted into the program, a process that could take years.[26] In fact, 85 percent of SSDI claims are denied at the first level and 75 percent are denied at the appeal level, according to the Employees' Advocacy Group, a company that helps process SSDI claims.

Applying for SSDI

The first step in applying for SSDI is to visit the Social Security Administration's Web site at www.ssa.gov or contact a local office by calling 800-772-1213. The representative there will walk you through the steps and explain what forms you need to fill out and the type of documentation (which is ample) you will need to provide.

If you do use SSDI, do not become complacent. Beware of getting caught in the rut of adapting your lifestyle to the meager government allotment. As I described earlier, there are many services available for people who live with a disability ranging from vocational rehabilitation to educational advancement. If you are well enough, take advantage. Even if you can't work regularly, if you sharpen your skills during the times you are able, when opportunity strikes, you will be ready.

YOU ALWAYS HAVE OPTIONS
Do Your Part to Keep Them in Tact

I would be lying if I said this whole work thing were easy. From getting insurance to the frustrating hoops we have to jump through for aid from our government, the issues surrounding employment can be incredibly difficult. When you get discouraged, remember: *You always have options.* If you are healthy enough to work, too sick to get out of bed, or somewhere in between, there is a resource out there, somewhere, that can reassuringly place you on a path to an easier life.

We live in a privileged country, where we have access to just about anything we desire. Think about people who live in countries that lack the most basic healthcare, social services, and employment opportunities. How would it feel to have nowhere to turn?

I know we each have hurdles to climb—but at least we are able to anticipate something better on the other side.

I encourage you to honor this fact by doing your part to keep our system moving in a positive direction. Get involved to help educate the public and our elected officials about chronic illness.

If you take that first step, you never know what might happen. I applied to California Governor Gray Davis for an appointment on the State Rehabilitation Council. After sending in my paperwork, I wasn't hopeful. I didn't have any political connections, nor had I served on any prominent commissions. But then—lo and behold!—I got a call from Governor Davis' appointment secretary, telling me I was in. For the past several months, I've been working on the council, making friends, learning new things, and most importantly, sharing my ideas to help make the system better. My guess is you have a treasure chest full of great ideas, too.

As you reenter the world, think about this: What can you do to get them heard?

5

LET THE GOOD TIMES ROLL

There's more to life than work. In this chapter, we're going to talk about having a good time again. When's the last time you went out with your friends? Went on a date? Had a romantic night out with your spouse? Now's the time to let go and reconnect with *fun!*

Happiness is a perfume you cannot pour on others without getting a few drops on yourself.

—Ralph Waldo Emerson

MY GUESS IS, it's been so long since you prioritized entertainment you've forgotten your old life, when you used to go out and have a great time. Work is important, but the other equally important part of life is *play*. Nourishing your playful self is a sure-fire way to build a Chronically Happy life.

You *can* have fun despite days filled with taking medication, going to physical therapy, feeling lousy, and, in general, managing your disease.

This may seem impossible, but, I can attest, it isn't. Before we get into strategies about *how* to seek pleasure again, let's explore your idea of "fun" and the reasons why it is important to keep it in your life.

FUN? WHAT'S THAT?

Discover What the Word Means for You

Everyone has a different notion of fun. Some people think it's zooming down a snow-covered hill on two planks of fiberglass at one hundred miles per hour. Others think it's going to the yarn store to check out the latest colors in wool. Still others relish the thought of cozying up with a good book or video. It's important for you to take stock and decide exactly what fun looks like for you.

You may be so sick and in so much pain that you literally can't remember what fun is. If this is the case, reach back into your memory banks and recall what you did to entertain yourself back then, before you got sick. Here are some questions to spark your synapses:

- What activity did you do that most relaxed you, that brought you the most peace?
- What activity did you do that most challenged you, that really pushed your limits?
- What's the best vacation you ever took?
- When was the last time you laughed, really, really hard?
- What is the best party you ever attended?
- What's the most entertaining thing you've ever done?

I know exploring how you used to have fun seems like a simple, maybe even a silly exercise, but really putting thought into these questions is very important. First, this kind of mind work helps you to remember what enjoyment is. When you live with a chronic illness, the unpleasant essentials of living—taking medications, going to dialysis, visiting the doctor, sleeping (you get the picture)—tend to take over, making it easy to forget exactly how to eke the joy out of life.

Next, answering these questions will help you to see that not every means of pleasure in your former life is off limits. Think about your answers to each of these

LET THE GOOD TIMES ROLL

questions. Could you do any of the things that brought you joy then now?

Perhaps you used to relax by strolling in the woods or soaking in a tub. Chances are these pleasures are still at your disposal. Even if you can do just one of the items on your list, why not bring it back in your life? The simple action of indulging in an old comfort has the ability to cover you in a plush blanket of worry-free memories, if only for a few moments.

Redefining Fun

The next step is to deconstruct your responses a bit, so you can reconfigure your old ideal of fun. Look at your answers and consider the ones that you can't do anymore because of your illness. For instance, you may have written "a food tour of Italy" next to "What was your best vacation?" Right now, a food tour on another continent is probably a stretch. The one you took to Italy was fabulous, but you most likely won't be able to take the one to France anytime soon. Accept this fact, and move on. I know it's hard, but try not to bemoan what you can't have.

Instead, replace the old ideal with something realistic. If you live near Napa, perhaps you can plan a trip to a winery and a French restaurant, taking special precautions to prepare for the long day. Take a course on Parisian cooking at your local community college, altering the recipes to suit your dietary needs. If it's hard for you to leave the house, buy a French cookbook. I know these alternatives aren't as exciting as a trip to France, but they are still ways of having *fun*—of shifting gears from feeling sick to feeling pleasure.

Fight the urge to compare your reconstructed version of entertainment with the rest of the world's. This woman suffers from chronic fatigue syndrome:

I can barely manage my daily chores. It makes me angry
that I can't do the fun things that others do. I hardly do
anything extra anymore. I just don't have the energy. I find
that I'm afraid to plan ahead for fear that I will not feel well
when it's time to go to the party, theater, etc. Is there anything I can do, or must I learn to accept the fact that sports,
socializing, travel, or just fun in general are no longer possible with a chronic illness?[1]

The truth is each of these modes of entertainment is
still possible, just on different scales. "Sports" may
mean joining a team that has players who also live with
illness. (Remember the woman who found a yoga class
especially for people with chronic fatigue syndrome?)
Socializing may mean having people over on your
terms, rather than going out. And travel may mean day
trips or short plane rides. While it is true your options
are limited, please remember they aren't altogether
gone.

No One Is Left out at This Prom

Each year I organize a prom for kids who suffer from
kidney disease. This is a perfect example of taking an
old ideal of "fun" and rejiggering it to fit a new set of
needs. Many kids with serious kidney disorders are
unable to attend school or, if they do, they often miss
out on its social aspects. It can be hard for them to
relate to their peers because they deal with life-and-
death issues on a daily basis. Not wanting them to be
left out of this important coming-of-age event like I
was, I decided to throw them their own dance through
my nonprofit group, the Renal Support Network. I held
the first annual in the year 2000 and soon discovered,
even though it wasn't *the* prom—it was better.

To find attendees, we forwarded invitations to all the
pediatric facilities in the Los Angeles area. They, in

turn, mailed the invitations to their teenage dialysis and transplant patients.

Not knowing what type of evening today's teenagers would enjoy, I consulted several students from Notre Dame High School in Sherman Oaks, California. They lent a much-needed shot of "cool" in the decoration and activity planning. More than two dozen volunteers worked through the weekend to prepare the Notre Dame cafeteria for the event. To create a Mardi Gras theme, we hung purple and blue crepe paper from one end of the room to the other and strung more than six hundred balloons. We installed a dance floor and a disco ball, and the Notre Dame teens made colorful feather masks for each attendee.

The teenagers began arriving at five o'clock, some in limousines, some in cars and vans. My heart began to race. I thought about the prom I'd missed because of illness. Now, I finally had a prom of my own to attend—and I was with a guy I actually liked, my husband, Dean.

In a room adjacent to the dance area, volunteers helped the girls with their makeup and hair in preparation for a glamour photo. When I peeked into the room, I watched them wrapping feather boas around their necks and trying on different costume jewelry.

Kids packed the dance floor as the DJ turned the tunes. A Michael Jackson impersonator ripped up the floor and later headed a Congo line. A Ricky Martin look-alike performed *La Vida Loca*. A kidney transplant patient jumped on stage with him and became part of the act.

One young man, Jack Freeman, drove more than one hundred miles with his parents to attend the event. Initially, not knowing what to expect, he was hesitant about staying beyond seven o'clock. He had such a great time, though, he was the last one to leave.

One of the teenage boys from Children's Hospital said, "I didn't know girls on dialysis could be so pretty!"

Toward the end of the night, I watched as the teens began to exchange their phone numbers and e-mail addresses, and I realized I'd accomplished my personal mission: to give them a chance to connect with each other at an event where they are often denied admission.

As the night ended, an eighteen-year-old kidney transplant recipient, Alan Brattland, told me this night made up for the fact that he hadn't been able to attend his school's prom. Before he left, he presented me with a white rose and thanked me for a very special evening.

Find New Interests

As you remember how you used to have fun, be open to the idea that you may need to start fresh and find new interests. Your body has changed, and, as a result, so has your mind. A changed mind often craves fresh forms of fulfillment. Here are some ideas that have helped me.

Become a Patient Rights Activist—This may not sound like barrels of fun, but surprisingly, it can be. Fighting for a cause makes you feel you are really *doing something* that will make a difference. It connects you with a community of like-minded people, and it has the ability to alter your mindset from "woe is me" to "I'm a fighter." What could be more fun than that?

The best way to cheer yourself is to try to cheer someone else up.

—Mark Twain

One way to start is by becoming informed on healthcare legislation. The Patients' Bill of Rights, prescription drug coverage, insurance reform, changes in the ADA and SSDI are just a few of the issues. Call a non-profit group that deals with one that interests you. Try the American Medical Association's Grass Roots Action Center,[2] which organizes activists on a number of health-related issues, and there are many locally based groups that lead letter-writing campaigns, rallies, and the like.

Spend Time with Kids—For those of you who don't have children of your own, and you want to awaken your sense of spontaneity and playfulness, hang around children. You must have a niece or a nephew you can baby-sit. Their parents will be more than happy for a break. Looking at the world through fresh, young eyes can be a surprising antidote to the sometimes blah-filled days of living with a chronic illness. If you don't know any kids, try volunteering as a tutor, or, if you are up for a bigger commitment, as a Big Brother or Sister.

The time I spent with the group of teenagers from the Renal Support Network prom is a good example of catching the enthusiasm of the young. I am amazed by these kids' bubbly, positive attitudes. It's so refreshing and uplifting to see sixteen- and seventeen-year-olds who genuinely want to better their community. It always brings a sense of joy to my day to be able to talk with them and find out about their lives and interests.

Get an Animal—I have two dogs, a parrot, and a cat. The unconditional love these pets shower on me has brought immeasurable joy to my life. I can't imagine life without them. It seems like my animals are always happy, and it takes so little to please them. A bone or a pat on the head creates excitement that is so spirit-lifting. The star of my menagerie is my African grey parrot, Johnny. With a vocabulary nearing three hundred words, and many of them rather cheeky, Johnny keeps Dean and me, and anyone who visits us, in stitches.

If owning an animal seems like too big of a responsibility, why not enjoy small doses by dog or cat sitting? Many Humane Societies also have companion animal programs that you might want to look into.

Get Involved in Your New Community—Almost every community has a strictly social aspect. You may find, as you get involved in your lupus education group that certain members go bowling every other Saturday. Hook onto that train. If people you've met don't meet socially, try initiating an outing. Sometimes it's easier to mingle with people who face the same set of difficulties you do.

> ### DON'T FORGET TO LAUGH—ESPECIALLY AT YOURSELF
>
> Okay ... here's another one about me. I received an award for patient advocacy a few years ago from the Independent Living Center of Southern California. A representative there presented me with a congressional flag and informed me that it had been flown over our nation's Capitol. Later that evening, I grumbled to Dean, "You know, I'm not all that impressed that they took a bunch of flags, tossed them into an airplane and flew them over the Capitol building."
>
> My husband patiently explained, "No, honey, the flags were flown on a flagpole *above* the Capitol."

IS HAVING FUN REALLY THAT IMPORTANT?

In a Word, Yes!

Placing "Do Something Fun!" on your to-do list (and checking it off, every day) is one of the most crucial actions you can take in creating a Chronically Happy life. Do not underestimate the importance of pleasure. It can be as vital as following your diet and exercise routines. For instance, research has shown that laughter improves the immune system by lowering stress hormones and increasing the number of lymphocytes that help fight foreign substances in the body.[3] And there is evidence that people who are able to connect socially or who have a positive outlook on life experience improved health.[4]

So, yes, it is important to put fun right up there with doctor visits. But there are more reasons than improved health to prioritize good times.

Pleasure Helps Shift Your Focus

For starters, a dose of entertainment can take your mind off your problems. Despite what most counselors say, sometimes denial is a great thing. Take yourself out and pretend, even for a few short minutes, that everything is okay. Go to a movie, have lunch with your friends, go to your local coffee shop, and immerse yourself in a newspaper. Take time every day to do something small to remove your mind from your body's limitations. As you indulge, actively fight off distressing thoughts by deeply involving yourself in what you are doing at that moment. Returning the movie to the video store can wait. Tell the pain in your back to go away. This is your time, and nothing is going to invade this space. Checking yourself out to relish in some small pleasure can have a tremendous regenerative effect on your soul. Try it!

A Little Frivolity Will Support Your Supporters

As you are well aware, you aren't the only one coping with the dailies of a chronic illness. There is someone by your side—your husband, your mother, your sister, your girlfriend—who has held your hand through all of this. It is essential that you two connect around something light, something other than your illness. Even a small helping of entertainment can be a boost to your support network. Something as simple as reading a magazine together and then having a lively discussion about the featured article can help realign the focus from your health to a topic more entertaining.

If you are having trouble justifying seeking pleasure when you feel this sick, or if you are simply too ill to enjoy yourself at all, try pushing through by thinking of the joy an outing will give your support person. (Know your limits, of course.)

Failing to make fun a priority can have major implications. Mandy Gordon, for example, felt terribly guilty that her husband had to return to work from retirement after she quit her job due to illness. He also had to take over the bulk of the household chores, since Gordon's chronic fatigue syndrome left her unable to exert herself. "I feel like I'm a nuisance to my husband and daughter," Gordon admits. Because of the extra work her husband has taken on, when it comes to having fun, Gordon doesn't feel she's entitled. "There's the problem of feelings of guilt, like, I'm supposed to be ill, I'm not really allowed to have fun, particularly when you're off work long-term."

Ultimately, however, Gordon says she's learned that denying fun only introduces yet another stress into her life and her marriage. Instead, she focuses on what she can do:

> I have tried as much as possible to be upbeat and positive, particularly in front of my husband and daughter, but it's not always possible to keep up the pretense. So there's been a lot of crying, both in private, and on their shoulders, and that's sometimes about the guilt. So to deal with it, I try to do one 'thing' each day. Last night I went to see my eighteen-year-old daughter in a musical she and her costudents have put on. I've also written a little Web site for family photos, too—fun, rewarding, and productive.

PUSHING PAST ROADBLOCKS TO FUN
Help! I'm Stuck!

If you are still having a hard time introducing pleasure in your life, perhaps you are tripping on one of the following stumbling blocks.

DIAMONDS ARE MORE INTERESTING THAN PAPER

One time I asked a woman what she did, and she replied, "I am a dialysis patient." This was at the top of her list! I asked her if she had children, and she replied, "Why, yes, even grandchildren."

I asked her if she baby-sat her grandchildren, and she said, "All the time."

This woman was many things: wife, mother, homemaker, grandma, cook, baby-sitter, avid reader. Dialysis patient should have been way down on her list.

If you notice that you have been defining yourself primarily on your health, it's time for you to get out and have some fun. You are a diamond that has many sides. The more you develop each of those facets, the happier, and more interesting, you will become.

Are You Doing What's Fun for YOU?

Funny, it took me a while to realize that I needed to spend my time and energy on doing things I liked to do, as opposed to pursuing other people's passions. As a young adult, I used to play volleyball with my friends a lot. Well, at four feet, ten inches, you can imagine that I'm not very good at the game. Despite the disadvantages of stature and interest, I spent many a Friday night playing volleyball because that's what my friends were doing. Now that I have a better understanding of what I enjoy, I realize I would've been better off staying at home doing something for myself and having the group over for dessert after the game.

Are You Letting Pride Stop You?

Part of coming to grips with having a chronic illness is accepting the unavoidable truth that the world will see the visual cues of your illness. You will be confronted with this reality when you begin socializing.

As you reconnect with friends, you don't want to be seen as weak, vulnerable, or different, but there is that pesky little issue of the handicap placard on your front dash flashing like a billboard printed with the words, "I'm broken!" Some people take their embarrassment—or pride—to the nth degree, letting it stop them from going out. To this I say: Don't be ashamed to use every single resource available to enjoy your life to the fullest. Following are some issues that may be holding you back:

Wheelchairs and Scooters—Even if you don't need a wheelchair or a scooter all the time, you may want to employ one for a big day out, where you know you'll be doing a lot of walking. Let's say you want to take your grandkids to Disneyland, but you know you won't be able to keep up with them. Wouldn't you much rather rent a motorized scooter than miss out on the day altogether?

Physical Appearance and Hair Loss—If your physical appearance changes due to your illness, don't let that stop you from having fun. Right before I had my last transplant, I lost most of my hair. What was left looked like baby hair. It was New Year's Eve, and I was planning on staying home, convinced I did not to want go out with my dreadful new hairstyle. A friend of mine, Steve, called me up and said, "I have an extra ticket to a dance, why don't you meet me there?" I went on and on about how awful I felt about my looks. He countered, "Well wear a hat or something. Let's go!" With his persistence I agreed. Wig on head, I arrived at the dance and found our table for ten. There was one empty seat, left for me. Nice-looking straight men occupied the other nine. I had the time of my life. I did not sit through one dance. And you know, the wig didn't fall off once.

Handicap Placards—Applying for and receiving a handicap placard can be emotionally distressing, especially if you don't show signs of being ill. Not only do you have to admit there is a problem, but you may feel like you are advertising your condition to the world. Also, it can be embarrassing when you hop out of the car, healthy-looking, and passersby throw you looks like, "Why are you in a handicapped spot?" To get over such feelings, I urge you to remember all of the difficult obstacles you had to overcome just to get dressed and get out of the house this morning. You deserve as many breaks as you can get. The government created these signs for a reason: People need them. There is no shame in being ill—just shame in letting pride stop you from getting out. In terms of the stares—take them as a compliment. You look healthy! That's great!

Mountains cannot be surmounted except by winding paths.

—Johann Wolfgang von Goethe

Incontinence—Certain disabilities can make it hard to reach the bathroom in time, causing mishaps in public. Although this problem may make you want to never leave the house again, a better solution is to be prepared. Make sure to visit the restroom first thing, at every stop you make. Even if you don't have to go, make a trip anyway. If you are still nervous, wear undergarments that will give you some protection. Nowadays such products are discreet and effective, and can give you just the confidence you need to relax and enjoy yourself.

REMIND ME HOW TO HAVE FUN AGAIN
Taking Trips and Other Fun Stuff

Now that we've recalled what fun is and why it's important to have it, let's come up with a plan to actually do it. Resist the urge to "throw out the baby with the bath water" and tell yourself, for instance, all traveling is out. Some traveling may be off limits, but you might be able to go to more places than you think, if you take the

LORI'S TOOLBOX
nine

A MALLET: *Smash the Barriers to Fun*

Perhaps fun is eluding you because you aren't able to get over the idea that you can't do the things you used to do. "If I can't go rock climbing, nothing is worth doing!" you think. If this is your situation, I challenge you to probe the real reasons you aren't letting yourself get out into the world again. Make a list called Barriers to Fun. In one column write, *I Can't Because*, and in the other write, *I Can Because*. Write down every single blockade you can dream up: I don't feel well, I'm too tired, I don't have any friends anymore. Go ahead, get it all out on paper. Then, in the I Can column, counter yourself. As you create your list, you'll notice there will be obstacles you won't be able to knock down. Set those aside for now; why worry about something you can't do anything about? Instead, think about the ones you can do something about, then work to make the change. Here's my list:

---

correct precautions. I travel all over the country, despite a sizable list of health problems. That said, I never jeopardize my well-being, and I am in constant contact with my doctors who are aware of and okay with my schedule. The same is true for other recreational pursuits. You can still do lots of things. Just be sure you proceed with caution and know your limits.

Traveling

The idea of traveling has always appealed to me, but when I was younger I rarely went on trips. I was always bound to some form of dialysis treatment—either three times a week on hemo, or every day with peritoneal.

LORI'S BARRIERS TO FUN

I can't because...	I can because...
I'm tired.	I can honor my body and take time to rest; I can challenge myself to use the "Acting as if" concept. I can know the difference between the time to push and the time to be still.
I'm in pain.	I can seek some relief through massage and mental exercises
I don't have money	I can watch the sunset, curl up with Dean, and laugh at Johnny.
I've got tons to do.	Laundry can wait. Life cannot!
I'm scared.	What's the worst thing can happen? (Maybe it's not really living, because I'm too afraid to take risks.)

Travel was expensive, too, and I never had much money to spare. These factors made the whole idea feel like too much of a hassle. Then one day I took a hard look at myself and realized I was a bit of a hypocrite. On one hand, I held all of these "Go for it!" personal convictions, on the other I was letting my disease stop me from trying something I really wanted to do.

After I had that epiphany, I made a vow to get out there and see the world.

Go For It...

I planned my first trip for one weekend; any longer and I would have needed to dialyse in foreign surroundings—too scary! As soon as my Friday dialysis was finished, I headed out, returning in time for my regular Monday appointment. On that first trip I went to Las Vegas. As I took more jaunts, I became increasingly daring. The most adventurous was a three-day cruise to Mexico, which left from San Pedro, California, on a Friday, and sailed to Catalina Island and Ensenada, Mexico, and returned on the following Monday morning. I had a great time. I danced into the wee hours of the morning and saw all the sights during the day.

If I can work around dialysis, I believe you can work around whatever it is that's holding you back from traveling. With a little planning and a lot of chutzpah, you can get out there and see the world, too.

...But Take It Easy

I slowly ramped up to my big cruise, and I advise you to do the same. Depending on your level of mobility, I suggest you start with day trips, then work your way up to an overnight, and finally a weekend. With each increment, you'll be able to gauge your comfort level, and you'll learn little tips that will come in handy as your journeys lengthen.

Plan Ahead

When I took my cruise to Mexico, I rescheduled my regular Monday dialysis treatment for a few hours later than normal, in case there was any kind of delay. Taking these kinds of precautions ensures a smooth journey and eliminates worry. If I had to rush from the ship to my dialysis unit, the last leg of my trip could have been ruined for the worry. Other tips:

Check on Insurance—A wise thing to do before you leave is to check on your insurance coverage's policy on out-of-town doctor/emergency room visits. This way, if an emergency comes up, you'll follow the proper protocol so you won't have to fight the insurance company later.

Research Accommodation—Educate yourself about where you are going. If you are in a wheelchair, for instance, make a phone call to find out about the hotel's accessibility. Before you leave for your trip, make hotel and restaurant reservations at wheelchair-friendly establishments so you aren't met with unpleasant last-minute surprises. If you need to refrigerate your meds, make sure you call ahead to see if the hotel has in-room refrigerators. If they do not have a refrigerator available, ask if you can store your medication in their refrigerators when you arrive—or, better yet, make reservations at a hotel that can better accommodate you. Another option is to have someone else do the research for you. Some travel agencies, like Medical Travel at www.adavacationsplus.com, specialize in coordinating trips for the disabled.

Carefully Plot Excursions—If walking is an issue, find out about parking at the theatre you'll be attending when you're in New Orleans. Will you be able to park close to the theatre, or will it be a hike? Find out if the theatre has a drop-off point, or if the management company can make special valet parking arrangements for you. If you are going on an all-day outing that will require a lot of walking, you may want to check into wheelchair or scooter rental. Plan day treks that won't exacerbate your shortcomings. If you know stairs are difficult, cross out the part of your trip to New York where you climb to the top of the Statue of Liberty. Take that time to go to SoHo instead. If you are traveling with a group, there is no shame in breaking off and meeting up a couple hours later. Why frustrate yourself, when there are so many amazing things on this planet to see?

Leave an Itinerary—Let your loved ones know you'll be traveling, and leave the hotel phone number and an itinerary. You should also leave your doctor's number and relevant insurance information. Why? If there is an emergency and you are unable to talk, whoever is your in-case-of-an-emergency contact needs to tell the hospital who your doctor is and how to get a hold of her. If you're on a waiting list for an organ transplant, tell the transplant center you'll be traveling and how you can be contacted. Time is of the essence! I happened to be on a camping trip when I got the call. I'm very glad I heeded my own advice!

Plane Trips

For plane rides, it's important to discover on your own what works for you. I always bring a neck pillow with me so I can rest comfortably, ensuring more energy when I arrive. Having arthritis, I easily become stiff. I try to reserve an aisle seat, so I can get up and stretch. My feet don't touch the floor, so I bring a little step stool with me. This helps to reduce the pain in my legs on long flights. Also, I try to stay hydrated by drinking lots of water, and I do not drink any alcohol while flying.

Another good tip when traveling by plane is to never pack your meds with luggage you are checking. Always keep them with you in a purse or carryon. You will arrive at your destination, but your luggage may not, and you don't want to be stuck without a critical medication. To avoid the embarrassment of a search, make sure you have a letter from your physician describing why you need the medication. This is very important for diabetics who require syringes and needles.

If your medication needs to be refrigerated or stay cool, purchase a thermal insulated lunch bag. These usually provide enough temperature control, even on longer plane rides. If you are concerned, you can probably refresh with ice during the flight.

THE MUST-HAVES

To date I have been to over thirty states. I travel for work even when I don't feel my best. I have an added advantage in that I can fall asleep before the plane takes off. I developed this skill after years of sleeping in hospitals in spite of all the noise!

As a veteran traveler, I have learned how to navigate airports, maps, and foreign surroundings. I've also learned to pack certain essentials in case anything goes wrong. I take these things with me every time I get on a plane.

Pagers and Cell Phones—If you don't have either of these, I highly suggest you get one or both. Cell phones and pagers have become necessities nowadays, especially if you are more likely to be met with an emergency situation. Call ahead to find out if coverage will reach your planned destination, and, if it doesn't, make appropriate arrangements.

Medication—Don't leave your meds at home! Make sure you keep them accessible and you take extra along in case you lose your planned-for dosages, your plane is canceled, or you need to extend your stay. I suggest keeping the extra in a separate bag, so if your carryon is stolen (heaven forbid), all your medications aren't gone with it.

Meds and Allergies List—In your purse or wallet, keep a list of your medications, including dosages and schedule. List any allergies you may have, including medications and foods.

Contact Info List—It's important emergency-care workers can find out how to help you. In your wallet, carry the number of your emergency contact, your doctor's phone number, and your insurance membership number. If your condition requires it, don't forget to wear your medical alert bracelet—the best way of communicating your health problems when you aren't able to.

Know Your Limits

Only you know your body. It will tell you when enough is enough. It's very important not to push yourself too far when you are away from home because getting help is so much more difficult.

Work with your doctor to know your limits, as well. Before you solidify your travel plans, discuss your trip with your healthcare providers. Find out what precautions you need to take or if there are any reasons you shouldn't go.

Be sure you mention where you are going, because the destination could alter your physician's treatment choices. If you are headed to the Mile High City, for instance, and you are a borderline anemic, your doctor may need to prescribe medication to increase your red blood cell count so you can breathe easier in the high altitude.

Eating Out

Even if you are on a restricted diet, eating out can still be a great experience. You just have to be a little more careful—and willing to make your server really work for his tip:

Be Specific in Your Instructions—Explain carefully to the waiter that you have a health condition that prevents you from eating salt, and that you can't have any, I mean any, on your potatoes.

Ask for a List of Ingredients—If you know precisely what you are eating, you can better regulate. If the dish you love contains an off-limit ingredient, ask if the chef can prepare it without.

Ask for an Off-the-Menu Meal—If you don't see anything you can eat on the menu, ask if the kitchen can make the meal you prefer. More often than not, kitchens can handle special orders; most people just don't know to ask.

OF PINE TREES AND PERITONEAL DIALYSIS

When I was on peritoneal dialysis, some friends invited me to go camping. This kind of traveling sounded good from a financial perspective, but I thought it would be out of the question. Curious, I asked my nurse anyway: "Is it safe to perform peritoneal dialysis while camping?"

Surprisingly, she assured me that if I had a closed environment and a means by which to wash my hands, I should be fine. So off I went. I did my exchanges in the car, which was parked near our beautiful campsite in Joshua Tree National Park.

The weather was pleasant and sunny, so I didn't have to worry about warming the bags.* Relying on the efficiency of solar power, I laid the PD bags on the dashboard. The first time I did an exchange, I took extra time and was extremely careful. Once I had the hang of it, it was a piece of cake! From that time on, I went camping whenever I had the chance. What might you do that you didn't think was possible?

* Never store extra medication in your car. Remember your car in the summer heats to astronomical temperatures, potentially making your medication ineffective.

Don't Be Afraid to Send a Meal Back—If you've made your request for no salt very plain, and you get a dish with salt on it, send it back! You are the customer, and it shouldn't be any problem for the server and the chef to meet your requirements.

Be Careful When Eating Out—Don't use the fact that you're at a restaurant as an excuse to go off your diet. This is critical if you take clients out to lunch or are on the road a lot with work. If a quarter of your meals are in restaurants, and every time you order you give yourself license to indulge, next thing you know you are out of compliance. If you must have the no-no, satisfy your craving by taking a small sampler bite.

Staying In

I don't think I need to say much about this because we all know how to stay in. All of us may not, however, make the most of those homebound nights. When was the last time you had a game night with your buddies? Never? Give it a try, it's fun. Here are a few ideas of things you can do with your friends at home:

Have a Poker Night—This is fun and easy. You order the pizza and provide the cards, and everyone else brings the poker chips or coins. The dealer gets to name the game; the longer the night goes, the crazier the games get. Forget about five-card stud, try seven card draw, one-eyed jacks wild, no peeky.

Organize a Themed Potluck—Two ideas: Grandma's Favorite Casseroles or Just Soufflés.

Host an Old-Fashioned Tea—Make everyone wear hats and gloves and serve little sandwiches, scones, and shortbread.

Throw Seasonal Parties—Have all your friends come over dressed up for Halloween and pass out candy to little ones. Host an Oscar party or a Miss America party. It's fun to eat chips and dip and make fun of all the dolled up celebrities.

Of course, fun doesn't have to mean there's a gaggle of people in your home. It can be as simple as hanging out by yourself or with your partner, watching television or a video, or, my favorite, surfing the 'Net.

> The most wasted day of all is that on which we have not laughed.
>
> —Sebastian R.N. Chamfort

Exercise and Sports

If you think your sporting days are over, think again. There are many organizations for athletes with disabilities. You never know what's out there until you check into it. The Paralympic Games, Athletes' with Disabilities' Victory Games and the Wheelchair Games are just a few. My favorite, though, because I'm often a competitor, is the World Transplant Games. Participating in such organized events is Fun, with a capital F, and has the added benefit of connecting you with like-minded people who are daring to stay active, despite their illnesses.

Danielle Campo's Story

Participating in group sports can be rewarding not only physically, but socially as well. For competitive swimmer Danielle Campo, seventeen, getting in the water liberates her from the body aches caused by muscular dystrophy and boosts her confidence. "I always feel like I have this sense of freedom. I feel like in the water I've never had any limits to what I can and can't do," she explains. Campo represented Canada in the 2000 Paralympic Games in Sydney, Australia. She won four medals, three gold and one silver. She also set a new world record in two individual races. During the regular season, Campo trains with an able-bodied, competitive swimming group.

She vividly remembers one of her first meets, the point at which everyone realized she had an iron will and a future in competitive swimming, despite her disability. Her inspirational story is recounted on the TransCanada Rally For Muscular Dystrophy Web site:

She was seven and entered a one hundred-meter event. Olympic-size pools, in which all serious swim meets take place, are twenty-five meters in length, so Danielle's race demanded four lengths of the pool. The only complication was that she had never swum any distance greater than a single length. With only her daughter's best interest at heart, Danielle's mother told one of the pool officials that they would have to help Danielle out of the pool after the

THE WORLD TRANSPLANT GAMES

By 1997, I'd won three medals in table tennis at the U.S. Transplant Games, and for my honeymoon, Dean and I decided we should head to Australia for the World Transplant Games so I could claim another piece of hardware. Fifty-one countries and nearly twelve hundred athletes participated in the games that year. Out of all those countries, guess which one I drew to play first? The all-time leader in my event: Japan. I won one game and my competitors clobbered me in the other two. My dream of a medal was shot, but I wasn't too bothered. The pressure was off, and the real fun, hanging out with the other athletes, could begin.

Just like everywhere else in the world, there are cliques at the Games. Typically, the hearts hang in one corner, the livers in another, and the kidneys dominate the field. The kidneys have a favorite break-the-ice question: "Where did you get your transplant? Living or cadaver?"

This year, I was determined to mingle out of my group. I made my way to the hearts and asked a transplant recipient, "Where did you get your transplant? Living or cadaver?" He wanted to know what kind of medication I was on. (See, you can't get a heart or a lung from a living donor. Unlike a single kidney, the donor really needs it!)

I was soon to learn, though, my question was valid. Also competing at the games were José Lopez and Keith Webb. Seven years earlier, doctors had determined that Lopez had an incurable disease and would need his lungs replaced. In simultaneous operations, Lopez gave his heart to Webb and received a heart/lung transplant from a woman killed in a car accident. Now, both in their fifties, they were competing against each other in a five-kilometer race. Neither of them won, but if one had, I wanted to know: Who would have gotten the medal?

first length of the race. At the end of two lengths a coach came over to get her out, but Danielle refused. When she finally touched the wall at the end of the fourth length, after more than six minutes—the longest time for that event in the history of the meet—exhausted and dead last, she was also thrilled: 'I reached my goal—I finished!' Although she had been in the pool alone for the past several minutes, Danielle had swum four times longer than she ever had.[5]

SWIMMING WITH THE DOLPHINS
A Lifelong Dream, Realized

Of all the animals on the planet, none understands playing more than dolphins. My entire life, I've looked to them as a source of inspiration, as a reminder that every day we have to laugh, to sing, to dance—to somehow experience the joy of living. I've always wanted to dive in the water and experience their world firsthand. As a two-year celebration of my kidney transplant, that's exactly what I did.

I headed to Key Largo, Florida, where a company actually lets you hop in the lagoon and splash around with real dolphins. After I suited up, the trainer sat me down on the dock, my snorkel, mask and fins in place, and gave me a brief overview of the dos and don'ts. Then she instructed me: "Be sure to lock eye contact with them." My heart was beating fast. I was a little nervous. These dolphins were larger than Flipper, but I took the risk and dove in.

Before I knew it, Dingy, with her endless smile, was directly under me, eye to eye. She did a complete roll and disappeared. When I looked to my right, there she was, waiting for me to grab onto her. As I reached for her dorsal fin, she started to glide through the water. She increased speed, and the waves sloshed me in the face. It was exhilarating. We circled the lagoon three times and then she dropped me off by the dock.

Moments later, the dominant female, Jeanne, picked me up. She was more aggressive and tested my abilities. She loved to dive, taking me down about four feet each time. I was able to hold on at first, but I started laughing and swallowed a lot of water and had to let go. I found myself quite a distance from the dock, alone, treading water and breathing heavily. Jeanne came up beneath me, just enough so I was able to sit on her. There I was, in the middle of the lagoon resting on a dolphin.

Of the three people in the lagoon that day, the four dolphins only interacted with me. I wondered if the dolphins could sense the staples from all my surgeries—maybe, in their unique view, I lit up like a Christmas tree.

To this day, I don't know if that was it, or if they actually understood that when I dove into their lagoon, swimming with them wasn't just a lark for me. I could actually feel the peace, serenity, and joyfulness of their undersea world. The experience gave me pause, and a chance to reflect on the many peaks and valleys I had traveled on my journey with chronic illness.

And I realized that I had many miles—many fun-filled miles—to go.

THE FOUR PRINCIPLES OF CHRONICALLY HAPPY LIVING

In previous chapters we've explored strategies to manage life with a chronic illness. There is a difference, however, between *managing* your life and *joyfully living* your life. In this next section, you'll learn four principles that will help you shape a Chronically Happy existence, one where you are no longer driven by the pain and frustration of your disease, but by the determination of your healthy inner will.

6 *PRINCIPLE ONE*

CONNECT, CONNECT, CONNECT

The first principle is the most important and probably the most challenging: making honest connections with yourself and those around you.

It is under-standing that gives us an ability to have peace.

—Harry S. Truman

Prior to meeting and marrying my husband, Dean, I secretly bought into the old line, "I wouldn't want to join any club that would have me as a member." Poor guy, I think of what I put him through in the early stages of our relationship. I told my friends he was dull. Not interesting. Predictable. He earned a pretty severe mental berating for the "sin" of wanting to get to know me.

I met Dean at a Toastmasters meeting. He showed up one night to check out the group, and I happened to be giving a speech about the importance of becoming an organ donor. He began attending meetings regularly. With each session, I noticed Dean maneuvered himself closer and closer, subtly tossing me "I'm interested" vibes. I thought, "What's wrong with this guy? He heard my speech. He *knows* I have all these problems. Why would he want to go out with *me*?"

Eventually, we made a date to play badminton. I have to admit, the sparks weren't exactly flying. I was used to riding a stomach-churning roller coaster of insecurity when I was dating someone. I had always been attracted to the ones who played games and didn't call when they said they would. Dean played no games. He made it clear from the start he was interested in me.

Though I reported to my friends the next day that Dean was the King of Bo-ring, the truth was, he scared the hell out of me. You see, I *felt comfortable* with the game players, despite the self-doubt they dredged up. With them, one thing was guaranteed: I wouldn't have to get too close. I could tell, even on that first date, there was no such guarantee with Dean.

Dean kept on calling, and we kept on dating. My feelings for him deepened, and I grew even more scared. I was convinced that he didn't "get it." For some reason, he wasn't seeing that I was Damaged Goods. I truly believed that, because of my illness, a man would always leave. So I tried something new. Rather than pretend the issue wasn't there, I pressed the point.

I sat him down and said, "You know me with a transplant, but tomorrow the reality is, I could be on dialysis again." I gave him all my books on the subject and said, "Read these, and *then* let me know if you still want to be with me."

When Dean came back, the just-read books in his hands, he said, "Okay. If you went back on dialysis, what modality would you choose?"

Dean went on to prove his faithfulness the following month when I checked into the hospital with a 104-degree temperature. My doctor feared I might be rejecting the kidney. Dean was there every day, being his solid-as-a-rock self. The kidney and I survived the ordeal, and Dean and I married on May 18, 1997.

THE IMPORTANCE OF IDENTIFYING THE TRUTH
Put Yourself First

The single most important thing you can do to ensure that you will live a happy life is to connect in an honest way. Easy to write down, hard to do. The reason it's so difficult is this: At the core of honest communication with others is telling the truth to you.

The story about Dean and me is a good example. I was running around informing everyone that Dean was a doorknob, when in fact he is a wonderful guy. When I did a little self-investigation, I realized I wasn't being honest. I was making up reasons not to like him because I didn't want to be rejected. I was afraid I was too imperfect to love, or once he saw how difficult a relationship with me would be, he'd take off.

Taking appraisal of your true internal motivations is something people spend years in therapy trying to accomplish. I'm no expert in this area. I can't give you all the tools necessary to dig down until you reach your personal truths. But I can tell you this: If you come from a place of honesty, your internal core will be content no matter what's happening to you, your body, or the world. You will be unshakable.

Fear: Where It All Breaks Down

I've noticed in my own life that the biggest impediment to being honest with myself is fear. I don't think I'm alone here, especially among those who have a chronic illness. Unlike our physically healthy peers, we have to digest life-changing information on a continual basis.

As a result, we have to make many more Big Life Decisions: Should I move so I can be closer to the best healthcare? Will I be able to continue my career? Should I have a child given the health risks? These are serious questions that bring to the surface our deepest insecurities. We tend to deflect such insecurities with non-truths, like "I didn't really want a baby anyway." Instead of making your Big Life Decisions from that fearful place, I encourage you to burrow into your insecurities and find the truth that lives underneath.

So how do you start digging? You identify the trouble. I don't know about you, but I have this fictional group of people in my head who tell me things like, "You're not good enough," or "You're not healthy enough to make it." I call this unsavory clan The Committee.

What's your committee saying to you? Are you not taking risks, like I almost did with Dean, because somewhere inside you believe The Committee? Here are a few more gems The Committee throws my way. Perhaps these will help you identify your own fears and stretch beyond them.

The Committee's Top Five

1. I don't deserve my loved ones' support.
2. (Before I met Dean) I will never find my true love partner.
3. I don't fit in; I'll always be an outsider.
4. My body will only deteriorate. Who's going to stick around for this?
5. I'll never have a good quality of life, so what's the point in trying?

When your committee spouts its Top Five, shout back, "Zip-a-lip!" Counter with the truth to stomp out the nonsense. Tell yourself that you are more than your body: You are a whole, loving, and worthwhile person who has much to give to this world. Remind the Negativity Crew of your vast accomplishments—and recount everything—even the tiniest of victories. For some it could be as simple as making breakfast. Counter what they have to say. To "I'll never have a good quality of life," respond, "According to what standard?" No, you won't go water skiing on the Delta every weekend, but you will have honest and loving relationships. And that's the best quality of life there is.

Moving Beyond the Fear

Once you identify and voice your insecurities, work with your supporters to *push through* the fear. After I identified my anxieties about Dean, for instance, I expressed them to him. I had a responsibility to myself, to him and to our relationship to speak with him candidly, rather than continue making him feel that he wasn't "good enough" for me.

Fear less, hope more; whine less, breathe more; talk less, say more; hate less, love more; and all good things are yours.

—Swedish Proverb

Marty and Gordon Lore are another example of two people who worked through their fears to reach a place of honest communication. Their heartrending story began when Marty was diagnosed with breast cancer in 1999. Complications with her treatment forced her to be virtually bedridden, and Gordon, her husband of thirty-five years, cared for her in their home for more than a year. Gordon describes his wife as "stoic and fiercely independent" and explains that she had difficulty discussing her fears throughout the struggle. Sadly, the doctors discovered the cancer had metastasized to her brain, and shortly after I interviewed Gordon for this book, Marty passed away.

Marty has always had a self-image problem and, I believe, was convinced I would not be there for her when she became chronically ill. For the first year, she fought any attempt I made to be her advocate with the HMO. Then she relented, and, slowly but surely, we became closer and closer. She began to realize I really did care for her, that she was someone worthy of receiving love, even of giving it. Taking care of her became my 'blessed' burden. It taught me the lesson of giving and expecting nothing in return, that true contentment comes not from receiving love, but from giving it. Then it returns, completing the circle of the wheel.

My challenge to you, in each of your relationships, is to connect in such a selfless and loving way. If you can set aside your fears and approach your loved ones with this kind of candor, then the first key to the Chronically Happy life is in your grip.

Step out of 'Roles' to Foster Honesty

Ahhh, that communication could be this simple: After a couple of intense sessions with your journal, you express your epiphanies to your partner or your sister and, voila!, you've got a great relationship. Sorry. It doesn't work that way. There's another person on the other end of the dialogue, someone who is experiencing just as many fears as you are. Like you, she is putting up defenses, building walls, and telling untruths to hide her own anxiety.

So how do you break through? Sometimes it helps to identify the ways you and your supporters are dealing with your illness. Following are "roles" I've noticed both patients and their loved ones take on to cope. Do any of these strike a chord with you?

The Ostrich—Ostriches pretend that nothing is happening, preferring to hide their heads in the sand. Gordon Lore said this is how his wife took the news of her breast cancer. "It appeared to me that she was in a (somewhat) state of denial, so did not ask questions when we visited the various doctors' offices," he explains. "I asked the questions I thought were necessary, but she resented it, saying, sometimes in the doctor's office, that it was her body and she resented me or anyone else making decisions about her body. I responded that someone had to act as her advocate since she did not appear to be doing so."

Marty's understandable feelings of denial made communication heated in the beginning stages of her illness, Gordon says. Her silence left her feeling left out

The most exhausting thing in life is to be insincere.

—Anne Morrow Lindbergh

of important healthcare decisions. Meanwhile, Gordon was feeling alone as he attempted to pursue the best course of treatment for her. It wasn't until she addressed her fear and let go of her resentment that she was able to trust her husband as an advocate, rather than an enemy.

The Victim—The Victim is best described as a person who cannot pick herself up and move on. It's unfair to have a chronic illness or to be a loving supporter of someone who is sick. It's normal to grieve the loss many times over. But when you can't get past that grief, a problem sets in. If she is the patient, she may let others "do" for her more than is necessary or reasonable. If you can identify, I suggest you attempt one small thing each day that your caretaker currently handles. As you accept more responsibility, you'll surprise yourself at what you can do. Your confidence will build, and so will your sense of independence. As you begin to do more for yourself, it will get easier for you to talk about your fears. Why? By taking action, you have already started to face them.

The Martyr—When a caregiver falls into the Martyr role, she tends to set aside her own needs to look after her loved ones, but then resents it later. My family has a few examples of Martyrs, and it's not a stretch to understand why. My kidney disease put them through hell. They had to place their lives on hold as we spent much of our time fighting my disease together. The problem is, for many years, they wouldn't let me forget it. They told me my illness was the reason they hadn't found satisfaction in their own lives. I still carry the resulting guilt, and many of my actions have sprouted from that shame-filled place.

After I recognized this pattern in my family, I delicately approached it with my mom. In emotional conversations like these, I always try to remind myself that my mother did her very best based on her resources. It's important to stay nonjudgmental because casting blame only deepens the problem.

If you see the Martyr dynamic emerging in your relationships, I suggest you talk about it, as I did. Let your loved ones know how it hurts you. I guarantee they aren't aware of their actions, so be mindful of this when you bring it up. If you approach the topic tactfully and with love void of resentment (remember, they're hurting, too!), everyone will benefit.

POLLY WANTS SOME COMMUNICATION

My parrot, Johnny, has an unbelievable ability to mimic *everything*. The car alarm, the cat's meow, television commercial slogans such as "Milk Does a Body Good," the phone ringing—even my voice. What he'll do is, he'll ring the phone and answer just like I do."Ring ... hello, whatyadoin'? ... ahuh ... ahuh ... yeah ... ahuh ... could you hold on for a second? ... Beep." (He does call waiting, too.)

Needless to say, having Johnny around is like having a tape recorder next to me, playing back my life. All day, Johnny lets me know what I sound like, and, I have to admit, it isn't always good. Some days, Johnny talks *a lot*, letting me know I could be doing more listening and less chatting.

The Overbearing Caretaker—When you are first diagnosed with a chronic illness, or are recovering from surgery, you really do need help. It is emotionally comforting and gives your body time to heal when someone is there to lighten the load. There comes a time, however, when independence becomes important again.

Loved ones who fall into the Overbearing Caretaker category can have a hard time with this transition. They prefer to dote on you, fluff your pillows, cook your meals, and, in general, make sure every tiny need is met. What darlings! How wonderful they are to tend to you so selflessly. But there is a difficulty in this set up. It has the potential of robbing you, subtly, of the very thing most central to your future: your independence. You *must* "do" for yourself, lest you become a Victim. Such a pattern is not always healthy for the caretaker, either. He may be gaining his sense of self-worth based on your neediness. When it comes time to pull back, it can be difficult because he won't feel useful anymore.

Although it may be a bit uncomfortable, let your caregiver know that you're ready to get back to "normal" as soon as possible. Talk in specific terms about the tasks you'd like to do for yourself, then make sure you follow through by actually doing them. Listen to what your caretaker has to say. It may turn out his fussing is grounded. He may be justifiably concerned that you'll take on too much. If you've been bedridden for several days, for instance, a walk by yourself may not be that great an idea. Open discussions are the first step toward mutual understanding and a workable compromise.

Pity Party Organizer—Even those closest to you may not know how to act when thrust in a caretaker role. This is especially true of the Pity Party Organizer. Your loved ones who fit in this category are most likely very sympathetic characters. You love them because they are so concerned, and they drive you nuts because they are too darn sad to be around. They want so much to help, but their words and actions make you feel like such a victim.

A friend of mine who has cancer gets calls ten times a day from a member of her family to find out how she's doing. Although she appreciates the concern, she wants to scream, "Enough already! Stop feeling sorry for me!"

For those of you who have loved ones who are throwing you daily Pity Parties, tell them you don't want them anymore. Let them know you'd prefer to be asked questions like, "What would be the best way for me to support you through this? Would you like to talk about what's happening and how you're feeling about it?" It may not be a very comfortable conversation, but I think it is necessary.

Another strategy is to ask the Pity Party Organizers how they are feeling. For one, this will move the focus from you. Next, expressing their concerns might unburden them and alleviate some of their anxiety. Find out why they are scared. If they are thinking Worst Case Scenario, let them talk about it. The reality is that everyone who deals with a chronic illness thinks about death. It's impossible not to, even if your particular disease doesn't have a high percentage of fatalities. Armed with facts, they may be less likely to treat you like a Fabergé egg.

CONNECTING WITH THOSE YOU LOVE
Don't Forget to Tend to Your Relationships

A faithful friend is the medicine of life.

—Apocrypha

Here's the bad news: No matter who you are, relationships take work, and when you have a chronic illness, they take even more. The good news is, your health can inspire you to form more fulfilling relationships with every person in your circle. Use the new mental perspective you've gained from your illness to strengthen the ties most important to you. Anne Fulton is a therapist in Halifax, Nova Scotia, and she works with people suffering from chronic illness. Fulton, herself, lives with environmental illness, a condition in which exposure to chemicals found in common agents, such as newsprint, cleansers, and perfumes, can bring on severe physical reactions, such as shortness of breath, muscle aches, fatigue, and headaches. She explains how ill health forces us to look more closely at ourselves and the most important relationships in our lives:

Illness and a hectic pace of life do not coexist well. Illness forces us to slow down, examine priorities, and make significant changes. We come face-to-face with the person we are moving too quickly to get to know on some deeper levels—ourselves. Our perspective can shift, often in amazing ways. It is this new perspective that may incline us to rework the relationships that survive our illness, so that they are deeper and more satisfying. With environmental illness, and other illnesses, it's not always easy to approach conflicts—if you're just too sick to do so, do not have the physical or emotional energy, or if the other person just really doesn't 'get it.' I've found illness usually shows you which friends really can be there for you and [lend] support in a healthy way, and which friends, even if well-intentioned, just can't. If your energy is limited, it makes more sense to save this precious energy for relationships that are supportive and easily workable.

As Fulton suggests, you will greatly need your support group as you ride the peaks and valleys of your health problems. The best way to make sure the network doesn't break down in times of crisis is to tend to it, like a precious garden, each day.

Your Partner

The most important plot of your garden is your primary relationship, which, for many of us, is our spouse or life partner. The stress of a chronic illness can threaten the lovingest of relationships, leaving both of you reeling at the time when you most need support. How can you tend to your relationship when you feel you have nothing to give? How can your spouse continue to treat you as an equal when he is also your caregiver? How can you connect, when this illness has taken over both of your lives? These are questions that come up for most couples as they face chronic illness. I can tell you from experience, if you keep the lines of communication open, you will get through this, no matter how difficult.

Remember to Empathize

First, you need to understand, I mean really *get* your partner's feelings. In the beginning stages, he is caught up in the same whirlwind you are, going through the cycle of shock, denial, anger, and depression that I addressed in the first chapter. It may help you to read that chapter again with this new viewpoint. As you read, see the loss through his eyes.

Take all these emotions and add one more—helplessness—and then you'll have an idea of your partner's struggle. This illness is yours, and as much as he wants to take it away from you, he can't. To make him feel included, *let him in*. Although you can't do many of the things you used to do, you can probably talk. You have a responsibility to be honest about your illness—don't exaggerate or hide the symptoms, including the emotional ones. The more you communicate, the less left out your partner will feel, and the less likely he'll be to beat himself up or to feel resentful later. Gregg Piburn explains how it felt to mutely watch his wife suffer, while he looked on, unknowing, in his book *Beyond Chaos: One Man's Journey Alongside His Chronically Ill Wife:*

> How can a man sitting in the upper deck spot an offensive lineman moving an instant before the center snaps the ball, but not detect that his wife has dropped into the funk of depression? How can a person take corporate-sponsored sensitivity training but be blind to the fact a loved one lives in fear of some nameless, faceless enemy? How can people get so concerned about the gnats buzzing around their heads that they often ignore the elephants bearing down on their significant others?[1]

Take the guesswork away from your partner by telling him clearly what you're going through. With a chronic illness, the straightforward approach is best; it's the way both of you will get your needs met.

Partner as Caregiver

When your partner becomes your caregiver, you are both entering into an unwilling relationship. This is not how either of you wanted it to go. Such a dynamic is rife with complexities, but, like most difficult endeavors, can have its rewards. It has the capacity to reveal unconditional love and can act as an affirmation of the patient's place in loved one's hearts. "Caring for my dear wife is not something I would trade," says Gordon Lore, who continued to visit his wife at her nursing home every day. "It made a better person of me and, I believe, has made her aware that she was really loved more than she knew."

The Lores lived with Marty's illness for three years. This type of acceptance won't happen overnight. First you have to work through the strife that caregiving can cause. One problem is "burnout." Fulton suggests avoiding this by sharing the burden of care. "You need to be constantly renewed in order to constantly give," she explains.

One Person Can't Do It All

It may take a while but, when burnout sets in, the lone caregiver is left feeling exhausted, overwhelmed, irritable, and more vulnerable to illness themselves. It's only a matter of time before the relationship between the ill person and the caregiver is stretched beyond a reasonable capacity. In the case of spouses, if this situation is left unchecked, the unique overtones of marriage can become so drastically altered that the magic that brought two lovers together can be seen sailing adrift on a distant horizon.

Pauline Salvucci, a licensed marriage and family therapist, spent ten years counseling family caregivers and people living with chronic illnesses.

> Spousal caregivers are often their own worst enemies, thinking they have to do it all. They don't put into the equation that they have to take care of themselves or they won't be able to take care of their partner. In order to take care of themselves they have to be willing to ask for help, know their limitations and create boundaries. In the case of married couples, it's not uncommon for women to take too much on. It's a mistake. The partner needs to be responsible for as much as he can. I coach a lot of angry, burned out, and frustrated women who waited too long before realizing they can't do it all. Becoming a parent to their spouse or sacrificing their physical and emotional health doesn't work.

Today Salvucci runs Self Care Connection, an Internet-based coaching business where she helps clients tend to themselves, particularly during chronic illness.[2] She works with both ill people and their caretakers. On her Web site, she draws a poignant analogy: "[Lifeguards] always put a life vest on themselves, grab their 'can' and connect it to themselves before ever venturing into the water to help the victim. Ever wonder why that is? They understand that you have to get yourself into the best position possible before you are able to help anyone else."

If you or your caretaker is burning out, one solution is to seek help. Self Care Connection is just one example of the many resources available to people in your position. Another practical solution is to have your partner give up some of the caregiving duties. Check into your insurance options. What kind of home care

are you entitled to? Can a physical therapist come in a couple times a week? Can a home nurse relieve your partner regularly during the day? Review some of the resources we discussed in Chapter 4 to see if there are any local nonprofits that can help you with grocery delivery, daily meals, or financial relief so you can afford additional in-home care.

Here's another action you or your caregiver can take that is a quicker, easier fix: *unplug*. Disconnect and unwind for at least a few hours on a regular basis. Take some time off to hang out with friends, go bird-watching, or veg out in front of the television. Whatever the trick, the best way for a caregiver to avoid burnout is to take care of themselves, too.

The only thing to do is to hug one's friends tight and to do one's job.

—Edith Wharton

Connect with Your Minds

How do you maintain a good connection with your partner when he or she suddenly feels like a parent? One solution is to shift your relationship focus from doing to thinking. Relate with each other where you are still able to engage—with your brains. Bring in outside materials to get your minds moving in the same direction—movies, puzzles, projects—whatever it takes. Work side-by-side on a plan to, say, remodel your house, even if a remodel is light-years away. Jotting down your dreams together will remind you that you can continue to look forward, even if your illness is pulling your body back.

More ideas: Each of you subscribes to different magazines. After you've both read your issues, swap. You read one article in your partner's and ask your partner to read one in yours. The resulting discussions will engage both of you and will affirm that you each take interest in the other's passions. You can also join an online book club together, or, in a more spiritual vein, you can pray together. Even if you don't believe in the same

RELATIONSHIP DEFIBRILLATOR: *Keep Love Alive*

I don't care how strong your relationship is, I can guarantee that its heartbeat will stall from time-to-time as you make your way through illness. When this happens, pull out the defibrillator and start jolting. Here are some relationship energizers that will leave you both feeling better by day's end:

Ask Questions and Listen—The single most revitalizing thing you can do for your relationship is to connect mentally. The key to connecting is asking questions and really listening to the answer. Ask anything, from "How are you feeling?" to "What are your thoughts on the city council race?" Doesn't matter. Having great conversations can be more fulfilling than physically connecting. The good news is talking is something most of us can do even on our bad days.

Recharge Yourself—Reserve your energy, sit in a park, take a nap, talk to a friend—do something to revitalize yourself so you have energy left for your partner.

Set Aside Your Illness—It's vital that you meet around something other than your condition. Watch the sunset, go to a spa together—whatever you do, make sure you don't talk about your health for a block of time each day.

Do Whatever Your Partner Wants—When your partner is also your caregiver, it is vital to give back. Pick a day where your partner gets to do anything she wants (she has a responsibility to pick something that you are able to do, too, of course). If that means you'll have to watch *The History of Spiders* on video and you have arachnophobia, so be it. You can cover your eyes.

Mind Your Manners!—This advice is very easy to heed, and yields great results. Say "Please," "Thank you," and "I love you" as often as you can.

higher power, channeling spiritual energy can help you relinquish your burden while at the same time bring you closer with your partner.

Accept Change

Just as you have to accept your life will be different with a chronic illness—in some ways better, in other ways worse—you both need to accept your relationship will change. If you continue to fight to make your relationship *what it was*, you will never be able to see *what it is* and *what it can be.*

There is a great deal of unmapped country within us.

—George Eliot

Christopher and Dana Reeve's marriage went through many changes after Christopher was paralyzed in a horse-riding accident in 1995. Dana, who is also an accomplished actor and singer put much of her career on hold in order to care for her husband. In a December 1999 interview with *The Westchester Wag*, Dana Reeve spoke about how she and her husband dealt with his new disabilities. "We don't have some secret formula that other people don't have. You need to find a place where both of you can grow and yet also stay together. It's about appreciating the other person fully—warts and all. I think if we hadn't been in that frame of mind from the day we got married, I don't [think] we would survive what we're going through now."[3]

Seek Help

Chronic illness can bring up so many difficulties in relationships, sometimes the best way to work through them is by getting outside help. Your doctor can probably refer someone to help both of you deal with the emotions of your illness, or you can seek counseling independently. There are marriage counselors who specifically work with couples coping with chronic illness. You may be able to find a support group that welcomes couples. You can go to your synagogue and speak to your rabbi. You can enroll in workshops, seminars, or retreats that cater to couples facing chronic illness. Whatever you do, don't forget to reach out. No matter how bad it gets, you are not alone; there are systems in place to help people struggling with exactly the problems you are facing. Use them!

Sexuality and Chronic Illness

I know that connecting sexually is one of the most important aspects of a loving partnership, but, frankly, sometimes it seems impossible. Between the medications, low hormone levels, irregular lab values, pain, and exhaustion, how can *we want* to have sex? This is a problem every couple coping with chronic illness confronts. It's tough for both partners—the one who is sick, and the one who feels neglected or denied.

David Axtmann has been on dialysis for thirty-three years. In that first year, when he and his wife, Marlene, were both twenty-seven, Axtmann struggled with his sexuality—to the point that his wife said she felt that the sight of her naked body "repulsed" her young husband. The couple took a proactive stance in solving the issue by scheduling an appointment with Axtmann's doctors.

"One of the greatest assets of our relationship is that we are able to discuss any problem," says Axtmann, who has been married to Marlene forty years. "In addressing this subject, we did find some good and necessary help." Axtmann's doctor said his troubles were most likely psychological. The couple sought counseling, researched ways to improve their lovemaking, and experimented with methods that would be new and stimulating to both of them. "Sex has never been the most important part of our love for each other, but it is a significant part. I feel it is a form of expression that should grow with a successful marriage," Axtmann explains. "The important issue here is that Marlene and I have enough concern for each other to deal with the problem, and not to spend the rest of our lives wondering about each other's feelings."

Like the Axtmanns, if you are having sexual problems, such as impotence or lack of desire, I suggest you talk to your doctor. Find out if the problem is physical or psychological. If it's physical—for instance your medication is lowering your libido—see if your doctor can help by adjusting the dosage. If it's psychological, don't shy away from the topic! Discuss it with your partner. Importantly, let her know that you find her sexy, but your body is just not working the way you'd like it.

Healing the Negative Touch Perception

For those of us who've spent a lot of time under medical care, an unconscious tendency to recoil at touch often develops, which can have a negative impact on our sex lives. The countless episodes of medical poking, prodding, and sticking have instilled us with a sort of negative programming. For many of us, touching is no longer a pleasure, but a sterile precursor to discomfort or pain, and, as a result, even a caring hug from a friend can cause us to become stiff and obviously uncomfortable.

To reprogram my negative touch perception, I slowly introduced pleasurable touch to my life. I began by getting monthly massages. As it turned out, these were more healing than I could have imagined. This ancient medical treatment offered a profound means by which I could enjoy a positive human connection and forget touch's invasive past in my life. Massage has made me more comfortable with all forms of physical contact, from a friend's reassuring pat to my husband's loving caresses. I am now able to relax and enjoy one of the most precious gifts one person can give to another.

FORMING NEW RELATIONSHIPS
Dating Advice from Someone Who's Been There

I know not all of you reading this book are getting through your illness with a life partner by your side. You are relying on your parents, your friends, and your siblings. These solid relationships are what will help you get through—but what happens when new people enter your circle? When you live with a chronic illness, going out with a new person can be more complex than it is for the rest of the world. Things can grow awkward if you disclose your illness sooner than you are ready. Dating can be a bear because of the negative self-esteem that often accompanies illness. And sexuality can get a little dicey: Do I tell him about the catheter after we've started making out or before our first kiss?

Having kissed a lot of frogs before marrying Dean in my thirties, I'm somewhat of a pro in this area, and I uncovered a few gems of wisdom—however unconventional—along the way.

Practice Dating

For many years, I proudly considered myself very discriminating when it came to the men I dated. "Why waste time on somebody who doesn't ring my chimes?" I figured. Then one night I was out with a group of friends, and we got into the inevitable topic of men. As I started with the familiar drone about there being no suitable guys, my friend popped in with, "Lori, don't you know the rule? You go out with anybody who doesn't give you the creeps." Letting this concept sink in for a minute, I finally replied, "Really?" She then went on to explain the importance of what she calls "practice dating."

Ask any professional pianist or baseball player, and they will surely tell you their performance directly correlates to the amount of time they put into practicing.

Makes sense. So why should the dating game be any different? For some reason, we have the mystical notion that when presented with an attractive individual and a free evening, we'll come out smelling like a rose. Well, for the extrovert with God-given social skills, a year-round tan and a rare sense of self-confidence, that may be true. For the rest of us, especially those whose self-confidence has taken a back seat to health worries, the going isn't so easy. We need practice relating to the opposite sex. We must learn how to relax around, be comfortable with, and speak the same language as our gender opposite.

Spending a few evenings "practice dating" with these non-Casanovas can help us learn the social skills and expertise that will enable us to be open and gracious when the "right" one comes along.

Also, with practice dating you open yourself up to people you may have passed by in your more snobbish days. I can tell you from experience, sometimes the practice session turns into the Big Game. As I mentioned earlier, Dean was one of those non-Casanova types. Not that he isn't cute. He's plenty cute. But I was used to a much more flashy kind of guy. You know, the type who flashes into your life, shoves your heart through a meat grinder, and flashes out again. Luckily for both of us, I had had the talk with my friend before I met Dean. He didn't give me the creeps, so I went for it—and look what happened with us.

You're in the Driver's Seat

Practice dating also helps build confidence. The more you go out, check out a person, see if you like him, see if you don't, the more you'll realize that you're in the driver's seat, deciding whether this person is right for you, rather than the other way around. So often with chronic illness, it's difficult to detach your sense of

MELROSE PLACE, IN A ONE-PIECE

When I was twenty, I lived in an apartment complex that resembled *Melrose Place:* lots of beautiful, tanned people living around a pool. My Melrose crush was with the star of the pool volleyball team. He was about as deep as his tan, but of course I didn't know that then. So when the time came in our relationship for me to tell him about my kidney disease—and to explain why I was the only one around the pool who wore a one-piece bathing suit (to hide my catheter)—I shouldn't have been surprised by his reaction.

"I've got something to tell you," I said, having finally mustered the courage to bring up the subject. "I'm on dialysis."

"Oh, man, I would rather die than do that!" he replied.

Doing my best to keep my composure, I responded, "Well it is a good thing I am the one on dialysis, or we wouldn't be having this conversation would we?" I rose up from the poolside chair and walked to my apartment, where I cried the rest of the night.

Clearly, this was *not* the time in the relationship to divulge my health status—not so much because of my boyfriend, but because of me. I was so insecure, I let his comment cut me to the core. I was unable to see it as anything other than a rejection of me, when I can now see it was a rejection of something he didn't understand.

His comment was flip, true, but in all fairness to him, it wasn't *that* bad. It just wasn't very smart. He didn't even know what dialysis was, and, because he was ignorant, he made a statement based on fear. In fact, once he understood the dialysis, he was fine with it, and we continued dating for a year after that.

So when the time comes to tell, test the waters to be sure your new friend is ready to hear the information. And, just as importantly, ask yourself if you are ready to face a less-than perfect response.

self-worth from the fact that your body isn't working the way you wish it would. Translate that to dating, and next thing you know, you're ready to marry whoever comes along. Meeting a lot of people helps you realize that your date is just as fortunate to be in your company as you are in his.

Practice dating can also show you that insecurities you have around your illness may be unfounded. After living with lupus for years and receiving a successful kidney transplant, Julie Glennon had anxiety about dating because she wasn't able to have children. She wondered if men would still find her attractive as a companion. Getting into the dating circuit cleared up her concern. "My thing is, I kept plugging away date after date. Surprisingly, a lot of these guys were really okay with this [the infertility]. A lot of them had dated divorced women with children and that was more of a headache. I found that it wasn't really that much of a problem," Glennon explains.

The bigger problem, she says, was determining the correct timing on disclosure. "I kind of drop the bomb periodically," she explains, laughing. "I always say the kidney transplant first, because that's 'kind of like' you're cured."

The Sticky Issue of When to Tell

Back in the days when I thought of myself as Damaged Goods, I had little or no discretion about sharing the details of my illness with anyone who would listen. In truth, my self-esteem was so poor, and I was so afraid of intimacy that I would tell every new date my whole story. I was living out my old self-fulfilling prophecy that said, "I can never really be loved because I'm damaged. And if you don't believe me, let me tell you about it!" As a result, I cried many tears over the men who ended up uttering the "F" word in my direction. "Lori, I just want to be your *friend*."

As the years passed and I became more emotionally healthy, I learned that such conversations needed to be reserved for the right setting, with a person truly interested in my life and my friendship. When I learned to

wait, I found having that discussion was one way to cement the new relationship.

That said, when it comes to getting involved with someone romantically, I don't advise you to hold off disclosure until you are seriously dating. I'm not talking the first date, but I do believe the person you are seeing has the right to know, and should *want* to know, the real you.

LIVE TRUTHFULLY
Strong Connections Will Follow

Whether you are striking up a new relationship or working on an old one, connecting boils down to one simple principle: *Tell the truth.* If you walk away with anything from this chapter, these are the words I want you to store in your memory banks and pull out again and again. In every conversation with yourself, your partner, your children, or your newfound friends, ask yourself if the words coming out of your mouth are matching the feelings in your heart. If they are, you *will* connect in a fulfilling way.

It isn't always easy to approach the emotions that come with illness with honesty, especially when they can be mired in so much anger, shame, and remorse. But if you do, you will reap lifelong rewards.

David Fulton had kidney failure and lived on dialysis for thirty-four years. When his daughter, Adela Robinson, was a little girl, she would lay her head on her father's fistula (the permanent access point for a dialysis needle).

He had two big ones on his hand. I would kneel by his bed, and my ear would rest on his warm, swollen hand, and I would listen. I could hear a thumping, beating sound. I would turn to my father and laugh. He would ask me, 'What do you hear?'

I would say, 'It's the giant, and he is walking up the stairs, his feet thumping loud.'

It was our little game. This was how I handled his fistula—that funny looking vein, which appeared on his hand and made it look odd and deformed, but was his lifeline. He never felt shy, embarrassed, or angry that such attention was brought to his disfigurement. He knew these moments built a special bond between us and, to this day, are some of my fondest memories of my father.

By respecting his daughter enough to approach matters truthfully, without fear, David Fulton's connection with her was unbreakable. It grew, steadily, until his death in 1998. Today Robinson's memories of her father bespeak the loving relationship they enjoyed while he was alive. I encourage you to let the truth lead you to equally fulfilling connections.

"I looked at him as one of the strongest and bravest man I ever knew," Robinson explains. "When I would see my father each morning, I would see him smiling with such a shine in his eyes. I'd say 'Daddy, what are you smiling about?' and he'd say, with his fist held high in the air, 'LIFE, LIFE, LIFE!' "

LET YOUR JOY INSTINCT RULE

Tap into your Joy Instinct and allow it to guide your life decisions.

Whatever you can do, or dream you can, begin it. Boldness has genius, power, and magic in it.

—Johann Wolfgang von Goethe

A S A LITTLE girl I loved to play with Barbies. I had the Barbie Dream House, the convertible, and the handsome Ken doll. Funny thing, though, even though I had all the props, I always made a special one of my own: an executive desk.

I constructed it out of my mother's old paperback romance novels. Barbie would sit behind *Temptation's Temptress* and make presidential decisions. *She* decided who ran the Barbie beauty parlor, who flew the Barbie plane, and who serviced the Barbie RV. She determined where and when she'd go out, and who she'd meet along the way.

No one questioned her decisions, and no one went on strike. She paid her own weekly salary, which included a clothes stipend put toward a new Day-to-Night Barbie ensemble with matching plastic shoes.

During those hours I spent marching Barbie around my bedroom, I was creating a vision of what I wanted the adult me to look like: A woman in control of her destiny, calling the shots, carving out a life based on what made her happy.

My dream of the future me was unfiltered. I let myself believe I would own a company, be the president of the United States—and marry Ken, raise a family, and live in a Dream House to boot. I hadn't yet discovered what wasn't possible. I hadn't yet heard it would be too risky for me to have children, or there had never been a female president. I didn't know that my dreams were limited because *everyone's are, and that's just the way the world goes, kid.*

In short, my vision of me hadn't gone through The Sieve yet. You know about The Sieve. *Dream*: I want to be an architect. *Sieve*: I can't be an architect; I don't even have my college degree. *Dream*: I want to be married and have children. *Sieve*: With my health problems, I hardly leave the house. How will I ever find a life companion?

As our dreams pass through The Sieve, what comes out on the other side is a watered-down version of what we want to become. Too often we just *touch on* our dreams, rather than doing the dream itself. In this chapter, I challenge you to step outside of the norm and *throw away The Sieve.* Don't just flirt with your dream once a year, once a month, or even once a day. *Live it* every single moment.

How? It's simple: Let your Joy Instinct rule.

THE JOY INSTINCT

What Is It?

If all time gobblers were stripped away—your doctor appointments, lines at the pharmacy, work meetings, car-pool duties—if they all evaporated, and what remained was The Perfect You, in a room, by yourself, what would you choose to do? Remember, this is you flawless, untied by the "I Can'ts" of this world, with no self-doubt and no health worries.

Would you spend time with your partner? Listen to music? Play a round of golf? Would you write or sing or dance or play softball? Would you do nothing at all? Or perhaps you'd construct an action plan to help protect the Alaskan wilderness, or maybe you'd work to end the conflict in the Middle East.

You don't have to envision just one thing. Envision one hundred. Think about the thoughts you'd have and the actions you'd take if you lived your life from a non-filtered place, a place free of health, money, self-esteem and relationship worries. In this room, determine deep within your gut what sort of mark you wish to make on the world.

Cherish your visions and your dreams as they are the children of your soul; the blueprints of your ultimate achievements.

—Napoleon Hill

As you do this kind of reflection, what emerges I call your Joy Instinct, your calling, the person you were meant to be. I believe every one of us has such a purpose, but the negative messages we receive throughout our lives block us from hearing it.

Before you can let your Joy Instinct rule, you have to listen to it. No matter how sick or alone or afraid you are, the Joy Instinct lives in you. What's it saying? Where could it drive you, if you let it?

Sometimes the Joy Instinct is hard to root up, especially when you are grappling with a lot of physical pain, but you can do it. In the end, the work will be worth it. A life built around your own powerful truth has no choice but to be happy, regardless of the burden an ill body brings.

Finding the Joy Instinct: Your Hidden Treasure

Calling out your Joy Instinct may not be new to many of you. Those of us who battle with health dilemmas tend to answer life's most essential questions earlier than is typical. Adversity has a way of pushing us, with a very

169

firm hand, into the deep waters of self-reflection. To those who have done this I say, "Hooray!" Pat yourself on the back for lifting the fog and finding your hidden treasure, the thing that makes you hum.

Then there are those of us who have been fighting so hard just to get out of bed each morning, the idea of living with purpose sounds a little crazy. "How can I let Joy rule when pain and frustration are my overriding emotions?"

It's true. The day-to-day difficulties of living with an illness are overpowering. But consider this. If you figure out a way to restructure your thoughts so they come from a meaningful base, no matter how much physical distress you are in, your health will become easier to manage. You won't feel like you are always fighting, fighting, fighting with your body. No, a shift in focus will instead push you to work within your body's limitations to fulfill the thing you were meant to do on this earth.

AN OBITUARY: *Do You Like What You Write?*

 If you're unsure of your purpose, some counselors or motivational experts suggest an exercise that can help you zero in: Write your own obituary. It may sound rather morose, but there can be great value in asking yourself, "How, specifically, do I want to be remembered in this life?" "What sort of legacy would I like to leave behind?"

Be as honest as possible as you do this exercise. Ask yourself the really hard questions: Will there be some sort of tangible evidence that I made the world a little bit better? Will my sense of kindness, honesty, persistence, and joy outshine my flaws?

When you are finished, if you don't like your obituary, ask yourself why. Consider what actions you could take to make it reflect the best you you can be. What can you do today to become the person you'd like to be remembered as tomorrow?

LORI'S TOOLBOX
eleven

What Will You Be When You Grow Up?

Another way to help define your Joy Instinct is to slip back into your childhood and recall your thoughts and emotions at that time, before the world started tossing "I can'ts" in your direction. Just think about me and Barbie; you can do the same. When you wiled away the hours in your tree house or submersed yourself in your bedroom after school, what did you daydream about? How did you answer the standard kindergarten question, "What do you want to be when you grow up?"

Think about people who correctly answered that question when they were six years old. You know who I'm talking about. The actors, business magnates, or

THE DASH

I read of a reverend
who stood to speak
at the funeral
of a friend.
He referred to the dates
on her tombstone
from the beginning ...
to the end.

He noted that first
came the date of her birth
and spoke of the following date
with tears.
But he said what mattered
most of all
was the dash between those years.

For that dash represents
all the time
that she spent alive on Earth.
And now only those who loved her
know what that little line
is worth.

For it matters not
how much we own;
the cars ... the house ... the cash.
What matters is
how we live and love
and how we spend our dash.

So think about this long and hard.
Are there things
you'd like to change?
For you never know
how much time is left.
You could be at dash mid-range.

If we could just slow down enough
to consider what's true and real,
and always try
to understand
the way other people feel.

And be less quick to anger
and show appreciation more
and love the people in our lives
like we've never loved before.

If we treat each other with respect
and more often wear a smile ...
remembering that
this special dash
might only last a little while.

So when your eulogy is being read
with your life's actions to rehash,
would you be proud
of the things they say
about how you spent
your dash?

—Linda Ellis

astronauts who explain to Barbara Walters, "Ever since I was little, I knew I'd be a movie star."

What do you think sets these people apart? Not much. It all boils down to just one word—belief. Most people say what they'd like to become. A select few say they *will* become.

Consider this: Most of us could easily fill in this blank: "I always wanted to be a _____." Very few of us could fill in this one: "I always knew I would be a _____." And therein lies the difference.

What did you always know you would be? Now, let's figure out how to be it.

Dreaming, Applied

W Mitchell is a businessman who lives between homes in Santa Barbara and Hawaii. In his fifty-eight years, he's amassed a fortune, traveled the world, headed a multimillion dollar company and served as mayor of a Colorado town, where his constituents called him "the man who saved a mountain" after he stopped a mining company from blasting a local peak.[1] Today, he spends most of his time spreading his inspirational message: "It's not what happens to you, it's what you do about it."

Our imagination is the only limit to what we can hope to have in the future.

—Charles Kettering

Mitchell has fulfilled his life dreams despite the fact that he is severely disfigured and bound to a wheelchair. He became paralyzed in a plane crash when he was thirty-two—that was four years after a fiery motorcycle accident had left him with burn scars over 65 percent of his body. Mitchell's is *the* story of pushing beyond physical limitations to live a joy-filled existence. How does he do it? It's all about attitude, he says. "Before I was paralyzed, there were ten thousand things I could do; now there are nine thousand. I can either dwell on the one thousand I've lost or focus on the nine thousand I have left."

Like W Mitchell, you can overcome physical adversity and live a fulfilling life. First, visualize what such a life will look like for you. Tap into your Joy Instinct to draw a mental picture based on what *really feels right*, versus what's not possible.

Describe the picture to a trusted friend. Where do you live? Who surrounds you? What kind of relationships do you have? What kind of work are you doing? Really see it as you voice it. Write it down. Read the paragraph often: Post it on your refrigerator, bathroom mirror, or your monitor at work.

Break It down into a Doable Plan

This paragraph is your end goal, your Big Picture Dream. It's important to always keep it in mind, but it's equally important to break the Big Picture down into a realistic plan. Your Big Picture plan will have many components: your relationships, your career, where you'll live, your financial future. Pick one area and ask yourself, what's the first thing I need to do to reach this goal?

Determine the steps. Stick them on a to-do list, and start accomplishing them, one at a time. I'm talking

about really simple steps. Don't put, "Learn to play the guitar." Rather, write, "Call the community college to find out how much the guitar class is," and include the phone number. After you make the call, cross it off.

Jotting down lots of small steps works. First, you'll actually finish them *because you can*. It's immobilizing to "learn to play the guitar," but not really that difficult to make a quick call. Second, a doable list reminds you that you are getting stuff done even when you don't feel well. Maybe all you can manage on a bad day is one phone call. That's okay. As long as you get *something* crossed off, you can feel proud to have moved one step closer to your dream. Use this method to determine what each of the major aspects of your life will look like in the future.

Before you create your Big Picture Dream, let's make sure you are building your goals based on your Joy Instinct. In this next section, we're going to talk about how to let the Joy Instinct guide your career decisions. For the purpose of brevity, I'm focusing only on the Joy Instinct and work, but you can apply the following ideas to all areas of your life.

CAREER AND THE JOY INSTINCT
Shaping a Career from the Heart

You've already spent some time unearthing your Joy Instinct. Now it's time to get a little more specific. How can you take the thing that consistently brings you pleasure and transform it into a way to make money?

Myra Schwartz always had artistic talent, but she never considered turning it into a career until she was diagnosed with kidney disease. As a sort of therapy, she started collecting beads in multiple colors, shapes, and textures and began composing them into unusual pieces of jewelry. Before long, she was selling her baubles, and, eventually, she opened her own business,

Spare Parts Jewelry. "When I noticed images of hands and hearts appearing in my work, I realized they were symbols of healing and love for me," she explains. "It was as if they had always been in my subconscious, but unavailable until I really needed them." Today Schwartz's business is growing and many of her items are featured in small boutiques. A major department store approached her recently to discuss carrying her pieces.

Like Schwartz, discover what kinds of tasks you do that deeply gratify you. Do you have a hobby that makes you lose the concept of time? Do you do any sort of work that helps you to come to terms with your issues on a symbolic level, like Schwartz's jewelry does for her? Maybe it's working with children. Maybe it's organizing events for your support group. When you find yourself in a sort of timeless zone, that's a good indicator you are pursuing something in which you have genuine talent and passion.

Here are some more questions that will help you draw out the Joy Instinct, as it relates to your career:

- What do you do in your spare time?
- What kind of books/magazines do you read?
- When you were in school, what were your favorite classes?
- If you are in school, what type of electives do you choose?
- When you look for a job, what section of the want ads catches your attention before you head to the area you have experience in?
- Where do you volunteer?
- If money were no object, what kind of business would you start?

Next, consider how this task or the answers to the above questions would translate into a career. If you love taking pictures of your two-year-old, for instance, what steps could you take to get paid for doing something akin to that? You could start by asking another mom in your toddler play group if she'd like her child's portrait done. Do a couple for free. Get her—and your other friends—to spread the word about you. Once you build your confidence, start charging. Meanwhile, you can join professional associations or take classes to make contacts. *Write each of these steps down* and cross them off as you complete them. This is how you'll shape your Big Picture Career Dream.

There are a million tiny steps you can take to make your career goals come to fruition. The key is *just doing them, one by one.* Be sure to undertake your to-do list at your own pace, though, keeping your health in mind. I talk a lot about *how* to find a job as a chronically ill person in Chapter 4. Once you figure out what churns your career motor, refer to that chapter for specifics on how to get started on your new career path.

Make Career Decisions Based On Purpose

Life has shown me that opportunities arise in the most unexpected places. It *never* occurred to me that I would edit two renal-care magazines, for instance, especially since I'd spent much of my career in promotions and medical-sales management.

> *Success is the satisfaction of feeling that one is realizing one's idea.*
>
> —Anna Pavlova

When I was approached about the editing job, I thought to myself, "Editor? Of two national magazines? You've got to be kidding!" I knew I could write, that I had good contacts and managerial skills, but *editing TWO magazines?* This was just so far out of my line of experience that I couldn't see such a thing happening.

Despite initially laughing off the proposal, the idea of actually taking the job started to slowly take root. For one, I liked the thought of using my creative skills. On a deeper level, however, I returned to the foundational issue of purpose. The place I find Joy is connecting with people and making a difference. What more effective way to fulfill such a goal than as a magazine editor?

While still mulling the job prospect, I had a strange thing happen at the Seattle airport. From a phone booth, I heard a voice, which I immediately recognized as a woman I'd heard give a memorable speech some

THE UNBEARABLE LIGHTNESS OF MICKEY

I can tell you the exact moment I realized I would walk away from promotions and pursue a career in the renal-care field. I was working at Disney Studios in consumer products/print production. In the middle of a design meeting, an argument broke out between the artists and the printer. They couldn't come to an agreement on what shade of purple Mickey's hat should be. You'd have thought we were deciding who the next president was going to be, that's how seriously they were taking it.

Then I had a thought: How many lives will be changed by the color of Mickey's hat versus how many lives will be changed if I shared my life experiences with kidney disease?

I devised a plan to tackle my new career that day.

months earlier. I respected her talent and wanted to let her know. After she hung up the phone, I tapped her on the shoulder. I was surprised that she remembered me from the conference. During the course of our conversation, I told her of my job dilemma. She told me plainly, "Lori, there is no question that you can reach more people with this job. Here is my card. Please send me your first edited editions of the magazines."

Sometimes strangers need to tell you what you already know. When I got home, I accepted the job, and have been working in the renal-care publishing field ever since.

I listened to my Joy Instinct and took the risk. Though I was leaping into a field I knew nothing about, I had complete confidence it was the right choice. I knew it would open door after door in my quest to fulfill my life's mission.

Talk Your Plan over with a Friend

Sometimes it's easier to identify and accomplish your dreams when you talk them over with a friend. For the longest time, I didn't consider incorporating my passion into a career. As a person with a chronic illness, I was just so grateful to have a job and medical insurance that I had never considered blending my work with my deepest personal truths. Then along came Eric Ward, a former boss. He used to have these lengthy "big brother" chats with me. He would ask, "Lori, what do you *really* want to do?"

I didn't know what to say, so I'd shrug off his question. But every now and then, he would raise the question again, "Lori, what do you *really* want to do?"

Little did he or I know, but those talks stirred the thought processes that eventually lead to a significant breakthrough. The head and the heart started working in sync, and I came to the conclusion I wanted to work in an area in which I was emotionally invested and where I would inspire people. The details didn't emerge until later, when a tussle over Mickey Mouse's hat made my life's plan come into focus (see previous page).

Do you have an "Eric" or someone you can talk to about your career goals and desires? Sit down and have that conversation.

Making Purpose Your Side Job

If you love the career you've chosen, but still crave a deeper meaning in your day-to-day endeavors, I suggest you use the talents you've developed on the job to fulfill your mission outside work.

If your calling is to help find a cure for AIDS, for example, but you have a satisfying job as an advertising sales rep, mingle the two. As an ad rep, you are probably pretty good at helping clients come up with marketing concepts. Volunteer these skills at your local AIDS charity. I'm sure they'd need someone to help put together brochures for their latest donation requests. Even if you aren't a medical researcher, you can still make a positive mark by using your talents.

I think one's feelings waste themselves in words; they ought all to be distilled into actions and into actions which bring results.

—Florence Nightingale

DREAM ROADBLOCKS

Stick with the Yaysayers ...

Once you've tapped into your Joy Instinct to identify what you want to accomplish in your career, surround yourself with people who believe in and can help you achieve your goals. When I first discovered I wanted to work in the renal-care field, for instance, I told my dialysis nurses, Jean and Linda. They went out of their way to hook me up with the sales rep, Jim Angelis, for a dialysis manufacturer. The lunch I had with Jim was an important step in getting me started in the field. Every little bit of help counts. And the people who are willing to give it to you are the ones you want on your side.

... And Don't Listen to the Naysayers

You'd think most people would be like Jean and Linda as you venture out on your new career path—especially since you have a chronic illness. After all, haven't you endured enough pain and disappointment to earn an enthusiastic "Way to go!" as you try something new?

A JAILHOUSE: *Keep the Dream Stealers behind Bars*

Dream Stealers come in many forms. Are you letting any of these stop you from accomplishing your goals? If so, stick them behind bars as quickly as you can. You have no time to waste letting negativity get in your way.

Lack of Faith—If you don't believe in yourself, who else is going to believe in you? Mel Taylor leveraged his faith to fulfill a lifelong dream: to write and sell a book. He accomplished the feat without any formal training as a writer. "Writing when I'm on dialysis, it allows me to escape to another world, a world where I can control the characters and the outcomes," Taylor says. "Writing is therapeutic. It is a wonderful place to go."

Taylor sold his first book, *The Mitt Man,* to a major publisher. He is in the process of writing his second. Had he listened to the voice in his head that said, "No way!" he wouldn't be doing his dream today.

Listening to the What-Ifs—What if I get sick while I'm on vacation? What if I'm back in the hospital right after accepting a new job? What if, what if? No one can read the future, including you. What-ifs are things that haven't happened. Don't let them play a part as you craft your future. Make plans based on what is in front of you, today, not on what could be tomorrow.

Looking Too Far Ahead—It takes a long time to bring our dreams into reality, and time isn't always our ally. It's easy to shelve a dream, reasoning your sickness will only get in the way: "What's the point of starting something I won't be able to finish?" To this I say, "Because you'll be living fully along the way." Also, you never know, a medical breakthrough could be on the horizon. Miracles do happen, every day.

I hate to say this, but just the opposite may be true. You'll probably run into plenty of people who will tell you your dream is too big, not executable, or just plain ludicrous.

Take Ed Masry, the levelheaded lawyer who gained national attention when Hollywood dramatized one of his cases in *Erin Brockovich*. He met negativity head on when he ran for Thousand Oaks City Council in November 2000. Masry has renal disease, and he discovered after he'd already started stumping for the position that he'd have to begin dialysis. A less hearty competitor would have left the race, saying it would be too difficult to run for office while starting a laborious course of treatment. Not Masry. Even after his main rival tried to rally against him, Masry didn't back down.

> The funny thing is one of my opponents in the campaign mailed all of the voters a statement saying I wasn't physically capable of running for office. I, of course, refuted that, and I think his nasty remark backfired. In fact, I challenged him to a race down the Boulevard. I would even drag my dialysis equipment and still beat him. He's kind of an overweight guy, and I knew I could run a mile better than he could. The newspapers loved my response and I won in a landslide. The reality is all of the voters knew I was on dialysis. I didn't hide it, and it certainly didn't affect the voters.

Like Ed Masry, people tell me all the time my ideas just can't be done. When I wanted to start the Renal Support Network Directory, negative-thinkers told me to drop the concept, claiming I would be violating people's confidentiality by placing them in a publication that revealed their medical conditions. Despite the opposition, I knew in my heart there was a need for the service. So I started consulting attorneys for advice on liability, and sure enough, the naysayers were wrong.

Today my annual Renal Support Network Directory helps patients all over Southern California link up with each other.

The surprising thing is, it's not just acquaintances who can be down-bringers. Even caretakers and friends fall victim to the "you-can't-do-it" mentality. They can become very protective, even stifling, after you let them in on your plan. I'm not sure why this happens. My guess is their reaction is rooted in fear; fear you might harm yourself, or fear that you'll be disappointed if you don't succeed. Or perhaps the person falls in the Overbearing Caretaker category we talked about in the last chapter, and he or she can't envision a life with a healthy you. No matter the reason, I suggest you talk it out. Figure out what they're afraid of and openly discuss the way their lack of support makes you feel.

Whatever you do, though, *don't listen to their negativity.* You can do your dream. I know you can, because I have—and all the odds were against me. No matter their intentions, the naysayers are Dream Stealers, and their words will only interrupt your passionate pursuit.

Sometimes the worst naysayer is you. It's tough to get around that nasty internal voice that says, "What, you're going to quit your job and become a blues guitarist? That's realistic." Many of us listen to that voice until it squashes our interests. This is especially true for those of us with chronic illness because often we can't afford to follow our dream—the drive to have a steady job with benefits is too great.

Listen to me: Just for a few minutes, quiet that voice and hear your heart. I know from experience it's worth it to take the risk and follow your dream. You may not end up playing in Chicago's House of Blues, but maybe you *can* start a band on the side or buy a guitar and start playing for yourself just because it feels good. And that in itself is a victory.

Reach for the Stars—But Pick the Right One!

While I urge you to reach for lofty goals, please make them somewhat realistic. Given your talents and resources, what can you accomplish? "I'd like to go the moon someday," probably won't work, but getting your master's degree in costume design just might.

Having dreams doesn't mean casting your common sense to the clouds. It means combining your God-given talents and passions with a little seasoning of persistent work.

As you reach for your goals, be careful not to take on too many at once. Remember, each dream takes a major investment of time and energy before it becomes a reality. Just like you tackle life one day at a time, take on one dream at a time.

CREATING JOY

How Much Can You Make?

Making decisions in your life based on your Joy Instinct, versus the fear, pain, and uncertainty of chronic illness has the power to transform you in unexpected ways. It can make the improbable possible; and it can arm you with the will to accomplish things you never thought were within reach.

And when you live with Joy, especially since you cope with chronic illness, your story will serve as an inspiration to those around you. Soon the ripple effect kicks in, and the next thing you know, good feelings are spreading like The Wave at a baseball game.

Jarrett Mynear knows a thing or two about bringing joy into people's lives. Mynear was first diagnosed with a rare form of cancer at two and a half years old. He has lived through six reoccurrences of the disease, multiple chemotherapy sessions, two bone marrow transplants and the amputation of his right lower leg. Despite his

If one advances confidently in the direction of his dreams, and endeavors to live the life which he has imagined, he will meet with a success unexpected in common hours.

—Henry David Thoreau

185

seemingly insurmountable health problems, the now-thirteen-year-old started the Joy Cart—a rolling toy dispenser that each week brightens the lives of the young patients at the University of Kentucky Children's Hospital.

Mynear first had the idea when he was six and hospitalized for his first bone marrow transplant at the Swedish Hospital in Seattle. He looked forward to the weekly visits from the "Pink Ladies," who faithfully arrived with small toys for Mynear and his fellow patients.

Three years later, during his second bone marrow transplant at the University of Kentucky Children's Hospital, Mynear missed the "Pink Ladies" and thought it would be a good idea to start a toy cart of his own. During his six-month recuperation, he and his mother sent letters to friends, family members, and local businesses asking for funds. They responded, and Jarrett's Joy Cart was born. That was in 1999. Since then, several hospitals have raised money for their own Joy Carts. Mynear's story has inspired a book, *The Joy Cart: The True Story of a Boy and His Toys*,[2] and he has been featured on *Oprah,* the *Rosie O'Donnell Show* and local newscasts in Kentucky. But the real reward for Mynear is seeing the excitement in the children's eyes when the Joy Cart arrives at their bedsides.

"It's not about the toys," he says. "It's about making a connection with other kids. I want them to know that someone who understands what they are going through cares about them—someone who has been through all of the needles, IVs, and tests."

By creating Joy in even the worst of situations, Mynear has lifted countless spirits—and not just those of the kids who receive the toys, but of the millions of people who have heard or read his remarkable story. Talk about the ripple effect!

If, despite monumental obstacles, Mynear was able to let his Joy Instinct rule (or in his case, *roll*), I wholeheartedly believe you can, too!

8 *PRINCIPLE THREE*

FIGHT PAIN UNTIL YOU WIN

Try a blend of mental and physical therapies until you can live with the pain. Don't give up until you find the formula that works.

I HAVE A confession to make. In my first version of this book, I left out the subject of pain. I didn't mention it once—as if pain weren't an issue for people with chronic illness. When the publisher read the draft he said, "Lori I really like your book, but I have one question. Why didn't you include anything on pain?"

The question threw me for a loop. How could I have sidestepped such an important subject? That's the equivalent of leaving flour out of a cake. So I sat down at the computer and asked myself, "What happened?" After a bit of soul-searching, I came to a realization. I was afraid. Somewhere inside, I felt that if I acknowledged the pain, I would make it real, and I would begin to feel what I've pushed to the back of my mind for so long.

If you live with chronic pain, you can probably relate. We pretend it isn't there so we can go on, keep moving, keep living. It's a strategy that works, so I'm not going to be a hypocrite and tell you, "Face your pain head on, you'll be a stronger person for it!" No. When it comes to pain, I'm all for denial. When that denial is mixed with a strong mental attitude, and, for many of you, the right medication, you will be able to manage your pain.

I've lived with discomfort for so long, I have stories about it that stretch deep into my childhood. My coping strategies were born in my youngest years, so that is where I'll begin.

MY JOURNEY WITH PAIN
Not Without My Favorite Blue Dress

I was twelve, and it was a hot August day. My mom and I were in a doctor's office in Pasadena. All of a sudden I felt very heavy. I wanted to lay flat on the floor. The doctor called my nephrologist at Children's Hospital, and he instructed my mom to get me to the hospital immediately. I dropped in and out of consciousness the entire ride, and as my mom pulled into the driveway, I opened the door of the moving car and fell onto the hot pavement.

I had on my favorite outfit, a blue sundress covered in big red flowers. As I fell, it protected most of me, but not my legs. They burned on the asphalt. I was aware of the stinging sensation, but I couldn't move my body. I lay still as a rag doll on the fiery ground.

The security guard rolled out a wheelchair, scooped me into it, and my mom frantically rushed me to the dialysis unit. She fought to keep me propped up as I repeatedly slipped down the chair, like Heinz ketchup slowly dripping out of its bottle.

At the dialysis unit, someone put me on the treatment table. I didn't feel any pain. But something must have registered because a few moments later, I looked at one of my nephrologists at the time, Dr. Christel, and said, "I don't feel right."

That's when my heart stopped, and Dr. Christel performed the CPR that would save my life.

As she worked on me, I saw the treatment room from above. Many healthcare professionals were feverishly pounding at my chest. I felt calm and relaxed, and I was not afraid. It was as if I were watching the television program *Emergency!* from afar. Then I noticed my blue dress all cut up at the end of the table. I became very angry. "Why did they have to ruin my favorite dress?" I remember thinking.

And that's it. The end of my so-called out-of-body experience. Maybe I decided to come back to mend my dress. Who knows? The next thing I remember is waking up in intensive care. I had tubes in every orifice of my body. My chest was aching, and the doctors were still at it, trying desperately to lower my potassium level—the lethal mineral that almost killed me.

When I awoke in intensive care, I felt strangely euphoric, despite the bruises on my chest and the overall pain. When I breathed, it felt as though fresh air reached the tip of my toes. In fact I felt so good, I kept trying to get up and leave. The last thing I heard was, "Give her a sedative so we can stabilize her."

I was able to shut out the pain. I, or the mental part of me, went away as my body experienced the discomfort. Where I went, I'm not sure, but I visited this place again later in life, after I received my third kidney transplant.

A Plea for Help

I was driving to my singing class. What a dreadful day it had been! I started the morning at half past four with four hours of dialysis. I had worked all day, and now I was on the freeway not moving more than ten miles an hour.

Seeing much, suffering much, and studying much are the three pillars of learning.

—Benjamin Disraeli

Dialysis was a regular part of my life now. It had been for twelve years and probably was going to be for the rest of my days—a hard fact to accept at twenty-three years old. The doctors had told me my chances of undergoing a successful kidney transplant were slim to none, and it had been seven years since the organ procurement agency had called me.

My life was riddled with needle sticks, infections, and an endless stream of uncertainties about my health. And on this night, I just couldn't shake the sadness. I knew I needed a fix, and singing had always been a way for me to release the emotional pain.

When I finally reached the school, the teacher called upon me to sing first. I agreed reluctantly. My voice was not much louder than a whisper, and I was trembling. The teacher said, "Lori, you're not used to being heard, are you?"

Her words triggered something in me that I had always felt. My way of coping was to ignore the pain, to hold back the fear and sadness. If I acknowledged these feelings, I feared the dam would burst and I would never stop crying. And that's exactly what happened. I broke down in front of my classmates and cried, the type of cry where I couldn't catch a breath. I never did sing my song. I had to excuse myself and leave. But the crying didn't stop. It happened again the next day, all day. I was in so much physical and emotional pain, I remember praying, "Please, God, help me!"

Though the plea gave me some comfort, the melancholy continued to gnaw at me. Maybe I need to connect with what is good in my world, I thought, so I turned to my friends, and we packed up and went on a camping trip. I was on my way out the door when I remembered something. I ran back inside and left a note on the fridge, saying where I'd be just in case there was an emergency at home.

Arriving at camp on Friday night, my plan was working. I felt a new hope in the beauty of the mountains, and I had a glimmering of that euphoric sensation I first experienced years ago, after my near-death experience, when my breath seemed to travel to my toes.

The next morning I was tossing around a volleyball with my friends, when I heard from a distance, "Has anybody seen Lori?" The woman was yelling quite frantically, and I ran toward her anxiously, sure there had been a tragedy at home. To my surprise, when she handed me the phone, I was speaking to the transplant coordinator. "Lori," she said, "I think we have a kidney for you."

I was in surgery that evening. The next thing I remember is waking up in intensive care on a ventilator. They told me I had had four respiratory arrests, and it was Tuesday.

The next two weeks were living hell. I had to return to surgery because my access had clotted, and every day the doctors and nurses prodded at me, trying to get the kidney to start functioning.

One evening, the doctors gathered around my bed and told me it was over. There was nothing else they could do. My kidney wasn't responding. In essence it was sleeping, and the chances of it waking up were very slim. Did I want to see a grief psychiatrist, they wondered, knowing this was probably my last chance at getting a healthy kidney. The match had been perfect. There was just something about my body that refused to accept this transplant.

"I don't know why you're telling me this," I shot back at all of them. "My kidney is going to work, so please leave me alone."

Once alone, I rubbed the area over my new organ, like I would have pet a beloved dog. "God," I said, "I know you wouldn't bring me this far just to leave me. Please let this work."

About an hour later, the room was very still and an eerie feeling came over me. I closed my eyes and started to weep softly. Then I felt a gentle touch on my arm. "Lori, are you all right?" I looked up and saw my close friend Bill. When I told him what the doctors said, he replied, "Doctors don't always know how things will turn out. This kidney is going to work. You deserve it. It's just going to take some time."

He held me in his arms, and I prayed and cried some more. After he left, I nodded off to sleep, only to wake up two hours later in disbelief. I had to go to the bathroom. *I had to go to the bathroom* even though I hadn't gone in twelve years. I rang the nurse, and she humored me by helping me to the toilet. A miracle. To my amazement and hers, my kidney worked!

NONPHARMACEUTICAL STRATEGIES
Use Your Mind and Your Mouth to Combat Pain

Everyone arrives at their own solution to pain. There is no one formula, and what has worked for me in my life may not work for you. It may help, though, to see the route I've taken, and perhaps you can learn a couple of short cuts along the way.

There are three crucial nonpharmaceutical elements in my battle with pain, as you can see from my stories. First, I allow myself to detach from my physical body. Since I've been fighting pain so long, I think I was almost born with this capability, but for those of you new to pain, such a method can be fostered through techniques like relaxation.

Next, I lean on my loved ones. In my darkest moments, I turned to my friends and family and said, "I hurt." Even though I know they can't do anything about it, just by giving voice to the pain, I feel better.

Lastly, I turn to God. I know there is a power greater than myself, and that Being, whoever it is, had a hand in the success of my last kidney transplant. I am not espousing any particular spiritual path here, or even saying you have to believe in God to fight pain. I'm saying that, for me, giving up my physical and emotional hurts to God works.

Find Spiritual Relief

A quick search on the Internet will tell you I'm not alone in turning to God during times of suffering. Web rings where members pray for the health of their loved ones (and strangers) abound, and there are numerous Internet sites—Christian, Jewish, New Age, nondenominational—dedicated to the relationship between spirituality and pain.

In the real world, hospitals have on-call spiritual ministers, like priests and rabbis, and lots of clinical studies have been done on the effects of prayer on healing. An article in *Paraplegia News* noted that "prayer is making a medical comeback. Given that 94 percent of Americans believe in God or some other 'higher power,' it is not surprising that 75 percent of patients think their physicians should address spiritual issues as part of medical care."[1]

Lisa Copen is the founder of Rest Ministries, a nonprofit Christian organization dedicated to helping people with chronic illness. She says she deals with her discomfort from fibromyalgia and rheumatoid arthritis by "finding purpose in the pain."

"When we open ourselves up to God's plan, the pain becomes bearable," she explains on her Web site. She feels her mission is to share her struggles through Rest Ministries, which in turn brings comfort to members of her group. "I have found a joy beyond description in being able to use my earthly weaknesses toward God's greater good."

But you don't have to believe there is a grand design to turn to a higher power to salve the pain. Simply praying, to whomever you see fit, can bring great relief.

A debate raged on the letters page in the June 26, 2000 edition of the *Archives of Internal Medicine*, a trade journal that publishes research and articles for physicians. The topic was a 1999 study on the effectiveness of "remote, intercessory prayer" on heart patients.[2] The research found that the patients who were prayed for had a markedly lower number of "clinical events" during their hospital stays. Letter writers ranged from those who took issue with the researchers' methodology, to those who lauded the team for tackling a difficult and underresearched topic. Fred Rosner, a doctor in New York, weighed in with this take:

> But does the efficacy of prayer have to be scientifically proved? Prayer can ameliorate or prevent despair and despondency. Prayer sets a psychological frame of mind to allow the body's psyche to be at rest with itself. Since ancient times, it has been known that the state of mind of a sick person influences the response to treatment. The general use of prayer as a modality of treatment for the sick is not in itself a prima facie argument in favor of the efficacy of prayer. The fact remains, however, that the majority of mankind prays for the sick at one time or another. The prayers may differ in content, in the manner in which they are offered, or to whom they are addressed, but both religious and nonreligious people alike offer prayers for recovery when they are sick.[3]

Prayers have a way of making us feel less alone, of making us feel that someone, somewhere out there, understands and will lend us aid. They let us hand over our struggle. They give us a chance to say, "I'm tired. You deal with it."

Talk It Out

Friends have a remarkable ability to do the same thing. As you fight your pain, remember what I did with my friend Bill as I lay in the dark hospital room, silently crying. *I shared my burden.*

In her healing practice using Jewish prayers and traditions, Marthajoy Aft says that most of her clients rely on family and community support to help manage their pain. "Connections are critical," Aft says.

"Occasionally I get an isolated person and they don't seem to do as well." In addition to using meditation and prayer based on Psalms and the Talmud, Aft will sometimes conduct healing circles with the families and friends of her sick clients.

Although the patients she works with do not always recover physically, Aft says the work they do with her and with their loved ones helps them to improve in other ways. "There's healing in the physical world, but there's also healing in the emotional world, the intellectual world, and the spiritual world. Healing does not mean curing. Some people have been cured of cancers or lived a better lifestyle while they were surviving; some people have reduced their use of meds or have found a sense of meaning."

Relaxation Techniques

Relaxation is another way to disconnect your mind from the aches and can be a powerful way to gain relief. Leslie Davenport, a holistic health teacher and marriage and family therapist, runs a program at Marin General Hospital where she leads hospital patients through guided imagery sessions to help them prepare or recover from surgery. She also helps her clients alleviate pain. She assists patients in focusing on an imagined "safe place," where they can direct their minds to escape the discomfort.

One patient recovering from cancer came to Davenport's program seeking help from the anxiety and fear that kept her awake at night. The woman was able to visualize her grandmother's farm as her place of peace and relaxation. "It became a kind of inner resource where, without me, she could return to," Davenport said.

Davenport describes her work with another patient in her thirties who was about to have a hip replacement surgery due to her spina bifida. Her surgeons wanted her to wean off her pain medication before surgery so she wouldn't be tolerant to the postoperative analgesics. Davenport used relaxation to aid her:

Real friendship is shown in times of trouble; prosperity is full of friends.

—Euripides

> I asked her to bring her focus inside her hip and to let an image form for how she experienced the pain or discomfort. She described in great detail a dagger that went into her hip. I said, 'Put your hands there and gently pull it out,' and she described a feeling of relief. She [also] described a boulder resting on her thigh, and she came up with the

image of a crane lifting the boulder off and experienced some relief. Her work was to revisit those images as often as she needed. It wasn't unlike taking a pain medication every four to six hours. Instead of taking a pill every four hours, you take a break every four to six hours.

A 1997 study backs up Davenport's anecdotal evidence that relaxation works. The study, conducted by the research arm of Britain's National Health Service, found visualization techniques helped limit pain in patients stricken with several different ailments, including arthritis, joint dysfunction, fibromyalgia and cancer.[4] Nine studies of 414 patients found that in certain groups, people who used progressive relaxation techniques scored lower on standardized pain scores than those who did not.

Evidence like this led the National Institutes of Health to sanction the use of relaxation techniques, including visualization and distraction (where the person focuses on something else to push the pain aside, like music or television). The NIH also deemed other types of non-drug pain relief, such as the mind/body methods of hypnosis and biofeedback, beneficial.[5]

Other Alternative Therapies

In addition to these, there are dozens of other non-pharmaceutical ways chronic pain sufferers can find comfort. Acupuncture and massage, for instance, have both long been lauded for their relieving effects. Many hospitals incorporate them in their treatment programs, and more and more insurance companies are paying for such services. I, for one, am a big proponent of massage—my monthly massage helps calm my aching joints and helps me disassociate touch with pain—a problem I've dealt since my youth.

Other methods to reduce pain are less widely known, but may carry just as many benefits. Some hospitals are

GUERRILLA TACTICS: *How to Get through the Bad Days*

When you have a chronic illness, sometimes the "bad days" are predictable, especially if you're on chemo, dialysis, or some other intense type of treatment. Sometimes they're not. When you are met with one, there is often very little you can do to make it any better. You just have to grit your teeth and get through. But there are a few activities that you can pull out of your Toolbox during these tough times that may bring some minor relief. Even if they don't, sometimes just taking a proactive step to get rid of the pain can put you in a better frame of mind.

Get in Water—Taking a bath, Jacuzzi, or a swim all have a way making our problems momentarily float away.

Get Outside—Even if you're just sitting on your porch or by an open window, the fresh air can do wonders for the soul.

Ask a Friend to Go for a Ride—If you aren't struggling with nausea, go for a ride to the mountains, beach, or the woods. The ride will provide a refreshing break, and plugging into nature can help relax your body and spirit.

Take a Walk—If you're up for it, even a short walk down the street will help. Exercise has long been known to help people maintain their health. Others insist move-

adopting laugh therapy programs based on research that hearty laughter inhibits pain. Paul McGhee, author of *Health, Healing and the Amuse System: Humor as Survival Training*, explains why. "There's about fifteen studies or so that humor and laughter causes a broad ranging strengthening of the immune system. Humor

FIGHT PAIN UNTIL YOU WIN

ment can also repair health. In *Healing Moves*, authors Carol and Mitchell Krucoff pen over three hundred pages on how exercise can cure more than twenty disorders.[6]

Accept Visitors—Accepting visitors when you are really sick may be the last item on your list of things to do, but sometimes a call from a friend can be the greatest boost. Companionship—and a distraction from your own routine—has the potential to be more powerful than any medication.

Hang out with Animals—Pet therapy offers a known benefit to the sick and people in pain. Hundreds of programs exist across the nation to train dogs and cats for nursing home and hospital visits, and lots of research has been done on the human/companion bond and animal-assisted therapy. According to groups like Therapy Dogs International and the Latham Foundation, animals not only offer entertainment, but they give patients a distraction from the pain, they promote social interaction, they relieve stress, and they motivate physical exercise.

See a Funny Movie—As we've discussed, laughter is a proven pain-reducing agent.

Create—Create anything. It doesn't have to be elaborate. It can be as simple as cooking a meal or singing along with your favorite CD. Tapping into your creative energy helps to get your mind off the pain and onto something that brings you pleasure.

And if none of the above suggestions work, remember: This, too, shall pass.

and laughter are really good at distracting you from pain. Some doctors believe it triggers the release of endorphins, but there is no evidence of this at this time."

Author and *Saturday Review* editor Norman Cousins first brought this notion to public attention in his book

Anatomy of an Illness, where he describes how he used *Candid Camera* clips and Marx Brothers movies to salve the pain of his ankylosing spondylitis, an excruciating disease that causes the connective tissue of the spine to disintegrate. "I made the joyous discovery that ten minutes of genuine belly laughter had an anesthetic effect and would give me at least two hours of pain-free sleep," he writes.[7]

As you can see, you never know where you'll find relief. Choosing the technique that is right for you is very personal and will require a bit of research and experimentation. For that reason, I'm not going to detail all the alternative therapies available to you. I'm just going to list a few of the more well known so you can get on the Internet or go to the library and check them out. Some methods may not work for you, but others have the potential to permanently change your relationship with pain.

- Acupuncture/Acupressure
- Massage
- Healing touch
- Hot or cold compresses
- Hot showers
- Hypnosis
- Magnets
- Biofeedback
- Sex/Orgasm
- Chiropractic
- Yoga

FIGHTING PAIN WITH YOUR DOCTORS
Get Evaluated, Get Relief

As I grew into adulthood, I started learning about all the options I had to control pain. Specifically, I spoke with my doctors, and I asked other patients what strategies they used. I also learned how to better describe my pain, so I could express my needs to my physician and get the proper relief. In the doctor's office setting, with so many things to go over, it can be difficult to talk about your pain in enough detail for the doctor to properly treat it. This is why I suggest you keep a pain diary and bring it with you on your appointments.

Doctors often ask you to describe your pain on a scale of zero to ten, zero being no pain and ten being the worst pain imaginable. Use this method as you log your discomfort so you and your physician are speaking the same language. Mark down the date, the time and the source of the pain. If you took medication, stretched, meditated, or tried in any way to get rid of the pain, write that down. Note what works and what doesn't, and whether your score on the scale increased or decreased.

You may even want to list the temperature and humidity factor. I find I have more pain when it is rainy out. Keeping a detailed diary will help you to mark trends in your pain and take proper measures to reduce it before it occurs. For instance, I make sure I wear tights or nylons to keep my legs warm when I know the weather will be wet.

Pharmaceutical Aid

Once you figure out how to accurately describe the pain, your doctor, if necessary, may prescribe a course of pain medication that will work the best for you.

While certain stronger pain medications can mean the difference between a poor quality of life and a good one, they carry their own set of complexities and side effects, making some patients and healthcare providers shy away from them.[8]

If you decide to use pharmaceuticals to control your pain, it is critical to speak honestly with your doctor

A WRITTEN NOTE: *Let a Pen Do the Talking (When You Can't)*

 Many of you won't have to deal with pain on a long-term basis, but rather in the fits and starts of your treatment. For some, "treatment" means surgery. Even though I've gone under the knife more than thirty times, I still get scared , and I always have questions. How much will it hurt? Will the surgery be successful? How long will it take me to recover? What kind of postoperative pain medication will I be on?

To ease my fears and to better manage my postoperative pain, I write a list of my preferences for the surgical team and tape it to the top of my chest. Here are some of the items I usually include:

Please Use Gentle Tape!—I ask them to back the tape of my IV and specify the tape I prefer. After one of my surgeries I had a fever, which melted the IV tape to my skin. Taking off the tape was more painful than the surgery.

Follow the Pen Marks—I mark the spot where I'd like my catheter to exit with a nonpermanent marker, and I indicate the position on the note. I don't want my catheter exiting where my bra strap sits or where the elastic of my underwear lands on my stomach. If you are having a catheter placed, but you aren't sure where to make this mark, draw your underwear and bra lines on your body so the surgeon can avoid these areas.

Play My Favorite Song—I list my favorite types of music to play in the operating room. The surgical staff will get a kick out of it, and more importantly, it will remind them that you are a person, not just a patient.

Keep My Family Posted—I remind them to tell my family of my progress.

Thank You!—I thank them in advance for their good work. It's the power of positive thinking! Use it!

about your medical history, the drugs you are currently taking, side effects, and any concerns you may have.

In many cases, people's concerns about pharmaceutical pain management are not well-founded. For example, some patients and physicians avoid certain drugs because they have an unwarranted fear of addiction. As a result, the patient suffers more pain than is necessary.[9] There are so many medications available, which can be administered in countless combinations, a solution that will work for you is out there. The key is collaborating with your doctor to develop the proper course.

Try, Try Again: The Key to Pain Management

My history has taught me an important lesson in controlling my pain. Try different solutions until you find the combination that works. This is true of all therapies: pharmaceuticals, alternative practices, and your mental attitude. We have so many options today, there is no reason you should just put up with unlivable pain.

Core to success in this approach is trusting your instincts. You may have to walk away from so-called experts and explore other options, as I did with my arthritis. I began having arthritic problems in my early twenties—an unfortunate result of having an illness so long. After a night of dancing, my knees would be swollen to the size of cantaloupes. I would manage the pain as it flared, by seeking injections of cortisteroids. This would leave my knees feeling young and free for a while, but then a few months later, the vicious cycle would continue. Anyone who lives with arthritis knows it enters your life like an unwelcome guest who is determined not to depart.

I started avoiding activities that jarred my joints. I'd only dance to my favorite songs when I went out.

During long walks I had to focus on each step. One mis-step could leave me laid up for a few days.

Eventually, my doctor referred me to an orthopedic surgeon—and it was a disaster. After an abrupt evalua-

BELIEVE ME, I KNOW FROM EXPERIENCE

When you've dealt with pain as long as I have, you dis-cover that a minor adjustment can go miles in quelling an ache. Here's what I do to cope; hopefully some will apply to you.

I Rest My Feet on a Stool—This helps with stiffness by keeping the blood flowing in my legs when I'm sitting.

I Wear Nylons in Cold Weather—This keeps my legs warm, which also helps with stiffness.

I Stretch—I take special care to move my body when I have to sit for long periods of time.

I Use a Body Pillow—By placing this between my legs while sleeping, I make sure I stay comfortably positioned throughout the night. I also have a good mattress.

I Buy Good Shoes— I also wear orthotics; both have helped immensely in alleviating pain in my knees.

I Exercise—Swimming is not stressful on joints, so for many people with chronic conditions it is the best option.

I Plan Ahead—This helps me to avoid getting hurt by moving too fast.

I Take Care When Lifting—I try to pick up items prop-erly, by bending at my knees, and I avoid lifting heavy objects altogether.

I See My Physical Therapist—Regular visits ensure I keep on top of my body's creaks.

Note: If you try these tips, please adopt one at a time, so if your pain is minimized, you'll be able to tell which one worked.

tion, he said I needed both my knees replaced. The news came shortly before my Australian honeymoon, where I was to compete in the World Transplant Games. The surgeon must have left his heart at home that day, because he sat emotionless, mumbling medical jargon about my x-rays as I cried. "I'm not ready for this type of surgery," I explained.

"Well, then, you should be fitted for braces. Until you're ready, there's nothing I can do for you," he replied curtly, stood up, and quickly left.

When I picked up the braces the next week, I was met with a set of neoprene nightmares that I could barely pull over my legs. I could wear only one at a time. Because of my small size, when I wore both, I couldn't stand up straight. It looked as if I had a corncob stuck up my, ahem, well, you know. I guess this was the surgeon's idea of preventative medicine. If I wore the braces, I certainly wouldn't have knee problems because I'd surely throw out my back. I thought, "If this is the expert's solution, I'm in trouble!" I decided there was no way he'd ever take a whack at my knees.

The next week at my chiropractic appointment, I explained what happened. Dr. Ramsey said, "I have an idea, Lori. Let me see you walk up the hall." I gratefully complied. She asked me if my feet ever hurt.

"All the time," I said. "I have a hard time finding shoes that are comfortable."

She prescribed orthotics, explaining that my feet were not properly supported, which was having a domino effect on the rest of my body. I cannot tell you how much the orthotics have helped me. The pain improved significantly, and I started to walk with more confidence. And, by the way, I didn't miss a step on my honeymoon.

FIND COMFORT IN A HEALTHY MIND
Once Again, Try Adjusting Your Focus

So much of this book has been about relying on your psyche to cope with chronic illness. Where our bodies fail us, our minds do not. And so it is with pain.

As I've said before, it may help you to accept the pain instead of trying to get back to that place of "normal." This is Cynthia Perkins' method. She is a mental-health professional who lives with fibromyalgia and chronic fatigue syndrome. "I believe that we can take a very painful experience and make meaning out of it," she says. "In spite of the suffering illness may impose on our lives, it may also help us to change, grow, and learn. My illness has challenged me to redefine my identity, my values, and my priorities, which led me to find deeper meaning in life."

Remind yourself of your powerful brain, your renewed trust in relationships, your fresh sense of who you are, your newfound spirituality. Home in on the positives your illness has brought, and the pain may be more bearable.

HEALING

When I say the mesa healed me,
I am speaking of how my hands turning
the pages of a book were drenched
in light, how the house where I lived

with its table and chairs became
as small as my illness
beside the mountains' blue-gray wash,
the desert's endless sweep.

The sky came bringing gifts
of iridescent blue, clouds and wind;
I was sheltered by its wings.
Mornings when haze still swathed the distances

I sat on the porch, breathing in
silence and feeling the presence
of all that is. On the mesa, I was granted
a reprieve from pain, from a world

out of balance that spells itself
within my flesh. In my heart I was whole.

—Marguerite Bouvard

9 *PRINCIPLE FOUR*

GIVE HELP,
TAKE HELP

Create change by giving back to the community.

APPLAUD THE writers and directors of the hit show *The West Wing* for having the guts to portray the president of the United States as an effective leader, who also happens to have multiple sclerosis. Until a few years ago, Hollywood writers wouldn't have dreamed of creating a fictional world-leader with a disability. *The West Wing* character shows perceptions are changing, albeit slowly.

The chronically ill and disabled have always suffered under the burden of negative public perception. People with physical limitations are weak, the stereotype goes, and they don't contribute to society. Franklin Delano Roosevelt, our thirty-second president, knew this. That's why he did his best to keep his paralysis tucked away from public view.

Today, well-known personalities such as Janet Reno and Michael J. Fox speak openly about their Parkinson's disease. Magic Johnson helped to tear down the AIDS stigma by telling the world he is HIV-positive. Mary Tyler Moore has been steadfast in educating people

211

about diabetes and prevention. Lance Armstrong, NBA star Sean Elliot and professional snowboarder Chris Klug have chiseled away at the sentiment that you can't be an athlete if you have a chronic illness. Rather than be sidelined by their diseases, these people have dedicated themselves to making a difference in the public's perception.

Whether you're faced with a mild or severe chronic illness, you can also help to elevate society's expectations of people with health limitations. You don't have to be a celebrity, and your scope doesn't have to be any larger than your own neighborhood. You can still inspire change.

Linda Dalgliesh lives in Winnipeg, Manitoba, where the extreme weather makes it difficult to get around, especially for people in wheelchairs and the elderly. Though she has fibromyalgia, myofascial pain syndrome, and migraines, she takes simple steps to help people in her town gain access to buildings. "I cannot change the world, but I am determined to change my corner of it," she says. If she sees a restaurant, bank, or shop that is difficult for a disabled person to navigate, she fires off a letter. "When something like this comes up, I think of all the hundreds of other people who cannot speak up for themselves, and I take action," she explains.

GIVE HELP
Create Change, One Person at a Time

So how can you help create a more positive public perception of the chronically ill? Like Michael J. Fox, you can start by telling your story. Let people into your chronically happy world, and they will see living fully with an illness is challenging, but possible; not only possible, but inspiring. Your lack of shame and can-do

212

attitude will have far-reaching effects in improving your community's perception.

And why not share? You never know who might hear your story and feel moved to contribute money or resources—or more—to make a difference. I have been interviewed a few times on the radio and in print, and most times, I end up getting a call from someone who wants to help. People love to make a difference. They just need to be motivated by a story that compels them.

Alone we can do so little; together we can do so much.

—Helen Keller

By speaking openly about his life, Mike Jones changed the course of it. Jones had been on dialysis for five years, patiently waiting for the call from the transplant coordinator. But it never came, and Jones was getting discouraged. He knew he needed a boost, so he decided to drop $650 on a self-development seminar. At the beginning of the class, he shared his struggle with kidney disease with a couple fellow students.

Later, as part of the class curriculum, the instructor asked everyone in the group to "make an unreasonable request" of someone. The classmates Jones confided in suggested his unreasonable request be to ask for a kidney.

He laughed off the suggestion, but the small group continued to talk about his condition. During this chat, Jones mentioned his blood type was O positive.

As the class wound down that evening, a woman named Patricia Abdullah approached him and said, "Mike, I am O positive."

Jones said, "That's nice, so am I."

The woman looked at him again and said, "Mike, I am O positive. Make an unreasonable request of me."

"And then it hit me," Jones explained. "I was speechless for a moment because I felt that the Lord was saying something to me through Patricia. I then walked up to her, put my hand on her side and said, 'Patricia, may I have one of your kidneys?' "

It turned out Abdullah's kidney was a perfect match for Jones'. In a strange twist to an already unusual tale, the transplant surgery was scheduled for September 11, 2001. "Our story gained media attention because the 9/11 attacks had raised the racial profile of the Muslim faith," Jones explained, noting that Abdullah was a converted Muslim. "The media was drawn to our story because there was so much diversity surrounding the surgery. You had a white Muslim woman donating a kidney to an African-American Christian in a Jewish hospital with a German, South African, and Jewish surgical team performing the operation. Talk about a rainbow coalition of people coming together to give the gift of life!"

So Jones got his kidney, Abdullah gave the greatest of all gifts, and the countless people that read their story in the days following the September 11 attacks were comforted, just a little, to know that good was still happening in the world. And the transplant community scored a few points on the education front, too, as readers learned about the importance of organ donation. Talk about a ripple effect! Tell your story. You never know where one little conversation might lead.

Reach out on a Broader Scale

Most people don't know much about renal disease or, frankly, any other illness that doesn't affect their lives directly. So, I have done my best to inform people through public speaking opportunities. As a result of my kidney disease and subsequent transplants, I have probably performed a hundred presentations, large and small, on organ donor awareness.

Blessings come back to me every time I give one of these talks. Sometimes it's the knowledge that I've inspired a person to talk to his or her family about becoming an organ donor; other times, it's understanding that I've changed a preconceived notion about how the chronically ill live. Most times, though, it's the joy I get from making people laugh when I tell one of my standby one-liners: "One positive thing about not having kidneys is you're a good candidate for a long car ride."

I encourage you to capitalize on your talent, whatever it is, to give back to your community. You may be shy, but a great organizer, for instance. Use that to your advantage. I have a friend who is petrified of public speaking, but she put together a poetry night at her local community center to raise awareness on her issue. She posted flyers and printed a small ad in the local paper. Almost a hundred people came out to share their verses.

Sue Gaetzman has lived with diabetes since she was a child. As she got older, she decided to combine her personal knowledge of diabetes and her writing and theatrical skills. Her play, *Blood Sugar*, premiered in Hollywood with her as the leading lady. Next thing you know, CNN, *People*, and the *Hollywood Reporter* were snapping pictures and doing interviews. Her perspective and optimistic attitude gained national recognition and she was able to improve the world's perception of this difficult disease.

You never know where your talents will lead and how many people you can influence by working within your skill set. And as you create positive change, the blessings will come back to you, tenfold.

Let Your Life Give Hope

As we've talked about in previous chapters, by keeping a positive mental attitude, you are sending a powerful message about the human spirit to everyone around you. Don't forget that you may be the only person your

If you want to be happy for an hour, take a nap; if you want to be happy for a day, go fishing; if you want to be happy for a week, take a vacation; if you want to be happy for a month, get married; if you want to be happy for a year, inherit a fortune; if you want to be happy for the rest of your life, help other people.

—Chinese Proverb

neighbor or friend knows who has a chronic illness, and you are representative of all of us.

When I met my friend Sheri Inglis-Schmikl, she was on the verge of donating her kidney to her mother, who had recently been diagnosed with lupus. Inglis-Schmikl was filled with fear about the transplant, so she sought me out to discover, firsthand, what the surgery would be like. Years later, she let me know how helpful I had been to her during that time, but not because I had done something spectacular for her. She said by simply witnessing my attitude, I had been an inspiration. It was one of the greatest compliments I've ever received.

We remain friends to this day. It's a mutually beneficial relationship, where I have deep respect for her as a friend and an organ donor and she for me as a transplant survivor.

TAKE HELP

It's All Part of the Cycle

In the years I've lived with a chronic illness, I've had to accept mental and physical help from my family, friends, my doctors, and, at times, even strangers. You may find yourself doing the same. For those of you beginning your journey with illness, this may feel a little uncomfortable. You may be too proud to accept these gestures. You may think, "I don't need any help! I can do it myself!"

I understand these feelings. I've had them all. I've come to realize that accepting the help of my loved ones is an important part of the spiritual cycle that makes up relationships. Accepting help isn't a signal of weakness or a giving up of independence. It's the first phase in a circle that connects me to other people. The next stage is giving back—to my family, to my friends, and, finally, on a grander scale, to my community. It's the giving back part that keeps us in balance and our relationships with ourselves and those around us whole.

YOUR SOUL, ON FIRE

My Wish for You

Nothing in life that's worth doing is easy and without risk. Whether it's accepting some of the challenges put forth in this book or deciding to go forward with an unexpected opportunity, there are risks at your doorstep beckoning a response. I encourage you to draw from your reservoir of inner strength and courage, and go for it. One of my favorite quotes is by Ferdinand Foch: "The most powerful weapon on earth is the human soul on fire."

Whatever your gifts or passions, it is my hope that you will continue to reach out to a world that needs the insights only you can offer. I want you to feel, all the way down to the soles of your feet, that you *CAN* make a difference in the lives of those around you.

And remember, the gift of your spirit is something that cannot be destroyed by illness, but rather divinely refined by the fire.

NOTES

CHAPTER 1

1. Elisabeth Kübler-Ross, *On Death And Dying* (1968; reprint, New York: Simon & Schuster, 1997).
2. Lance Armstrong, *It's Not About the Bike: My Journey Back to Life* (New York: Berkeley Books, 2000), 14.
3. Armstrong, 5.
4. For more information on arthritis see Jason Theodosakis, Barry Fox, and Brenda D. Adderly, *The Arthritis Cure: The Medical Miracle That Can Halt, Reverse and May Even Cure Osteoarthritis* (New York: St Martin's Griffin, 1996).
5. Les Carter, Frank Minirth, and Paul Meier, *The Anger Workbook* (Nashville: Thomas Nelson Publishers, 1993).
6. Ahmed Samei Huda, "Depression and Physical Illness," NetDoctor, Internet, February 2000. Available: http://www.netdoctor.co.uk.
7. Lee Shirey, "Depression: A Treatable Disease," National Academy on an Aging Society's series *Challenges for the 21st Century: Chronic and Disabling Conditions*, no. 9 (July 2000): 1.
8. Arthur Rifkin, "Depression in physically ill patients: Don't dismiss it as 'understandable,'" *Postgrad Medicine,* vol. 92, no. 3 (September 1, 1992): 154.
9. American Psychiatric Association, *Diagnostic and Statistical Manual of Mental Disorders*, 4th ed. (Washington, D.C.: American Psychiatric Association, 2000).
10. Rifkin, 147.
11. See note 7 above.

CHAPTER 2

1. Richard Lederer, *Fractured English: A Pleasury of Bloopers and Blunders, Fluffs and Flubs, and Gaffes and Goofs* (New York: Pocket Books, a division of Simon & Schuster, 1996), 71–74. Lederer cites *Sic Humor*, "a collection of bloopers from medical transcription," edited by Diane S. Heath, as his source for the bloopers that appear here.

2. The Patient's Guide to Healthcare Information on the Internet, front page, Internet, June 6, 2002.Available:www3.telus.net/me/patientsguide.

CHAPTER 3

1. Lee S. Berk, David L. Felten, Stanley A. Tan, Barry B. Bittman, and James Westengard, "Moducation of Neuroimmune Parameters During The Eustress of Humor-Associated Mirthful Laughter," *Alternative Therapies,* vol. 7, no. 2, (March 2001): 62–76.

2. A.J.S. Rayl, "Humor: A Mind-Body Connection," *The Scientist,* vol. 14, no. 19, (October 2, 2000): 1.

3. Berk, et al., 62.

4. Paul E. McGhee, *Health, Healing and the Amuse System: Humor As Survival Training* (Dubuque, Iowa: Kendall/Hunt Publishing, 1999).

5. For more information about these speakers, log on to www.LesBrown.com, www.DrWayneDyer.com, or www.marianne.com, respectively.

6. David D. Burns, *Intimate Connections* (New York: New American Library, 1985).

7. Burns' question paraphrased for simplicity.

8. Burns' question paraphrased for simplicity.

9. Shakti Gawain, *Creative Visualizations* (Novato: New World Library, 1995), 31–33.

10. Suzanne Falter-Barnes, *How Much Joy Can You Stand: A Creative Guide to Facing Your Fears and Making Your Dreams Come True* (New York: Ballantine Wellspring, 2000).

11. Bill Gottlieb, et al., *New Choices in Natural Healing: Over 1,800 of the Best Self-Help Remedies from the World of Alternative Medicine* (Emmaus, Pennsylvania: Rodale, Inc., 1995), 85–88.

12. Carol Krucoff, Mitchell Krucoff, Adam Brill, *Healing Moves: How To Cure, Relieve, And Prevent Common Ailments With Exercise* (New York: Harmony Books, 2000).

13. Carol Krucoff and Mitchell Krucoff, "Movement is Medicine: Nine Steps To Help Harness the Healing Power of Physical Activity," Healing Well, Internet, April–May 2001. Available: http://www.healingwell.com/library/health/krucoff1.asp.

CHAPTER 4

1. Audrey Kron, *Meeting The Challenge: Living With Chronic Illness* (Detroit: Audrey Kron, 1996), 156.

2. Joan Friedlander, "Remission with Crohn's Disease: Beyond Medicine, Life-Long Lessons from a Chronic Illness," Imagined Life, Internet, May 2001. For more information on Joan Friedlander's practice, go to her Web site at www.imaginedlife.com.

3. Robert J. Mills, "Health Insurance Coverage: 2000," U.S. Census Bureau's *Current Population Reports* (September 2001): 2. According to the same study, 24.2 percent of the population had state-funded insurance, and 14 percent had no health coverage at all.

4. *Americans with Disabilities Act*, U.S. Code, title 42, chapter 126, sec. 12102 (1990). Specifically, the ADA defines "disability" as "a physical or mental impairment that substantially limits one or more of the major life activities of such individual; a record of such an impairment; or being regarded as having such an impairment."

5. U.S. Equal Employment Opportunity Commission and U.S. Department of Justice, "Americans with Disabilities Questions and Answers," U.S. Department of Justice ADA Web site, Internet, January 18, 2002. Available: http://www.usdoj.gov/crt/ada/qandaeng.htm.

6. *Americans with Disabilities Act*, sec. 12112.

7. Patient Advocate Foundation, *First My Illness, Now Job Discrimination: Steps to Resolution* (Newport News: Patient Advocate Foundation, 2000), 15.

8. *Americans with Disabilities Act*, sec. 12111.

9. Patient Advocate Foundation, *First My Illness*, 15–16. *First My Illness* further explains, "Undue hardship would be changes to the work environment that would include significant difficulty and/or expense. Undue hardship also refers to accommodation that would be disruptive or that would alter the nature of the business. Each case of 'reasonable accommodation' or employ ers' charge of 'undue hardship' would be handled on a case by case basis."

10. U.S. Department of Justice Civil Rights Division, "Baltimore City Schools Agree to Pay Blind Teacher $55,000 to Settle Title I Discrimination Suit," U.S. Department of Justice Civil Rights Division Web site, Disability Rights section, Internet,

October–December 2001. Available:
http://www.usdoj.gov/crt/ada/octdec01.htm.

11. *Family Medical Leave Act*, U.S. Code, title 29, chapter 28, sec. 2612 (1993).

12. *Family Medical Leave Act*, sec. 2611.

13. Patient Advocate Foundation, *First My Illness*, 16–18.

14. Patient Advocate Foundation, *First My Illness*, 16.

15. Patient Advocate Foundation, *First My Illness*, 17.

16. The U.S. Equal Employment Opportunity Commission, "Federal Laws Prohibiting Job Discrimination, Questions and Answers," The U.S. Equal Employment Opportunity Commission Web site, Internet, June 27, 2001. Available: http://www.eeoc.gov/facts/qanda.html.

17. Health Insurance Portability and Accountability Act, Public Law 104–191, 104th Cong. (August 21, 1996).

18. According to the Centers for Medicaid and Medicare Services, the organization that oversees the HIPAA, "a preexisting condition is any medical condition, physical or mental, that you have before health coverage begins. The cause of the condition does not matter and could be the result of an accident or illness." Available: http://www.hcfa.gov/medicaid//hipaa/online/010651.asp.

19. U.S. Department of Health and Human Services and Health Care Financing Administration, *Protecting Your Health Insurance Coverage* (Baltimore: U.S. Department of Health and Human Services, September 2000), 2–3, 7.

20. Kevin T. Stroupe, Eleanor D. Kinney, and Thomas J. Kniesner, "Does Chronic Illness Affect the Adequacy of Health Insurance Coverage?" *CPR Working Paper Series*, Maxwell School of Citizenship and Public Affairs, Syracuse University, no. 20 (March 2000): 4.

21. U.S. Department of Health and Human Services, *Protecting Your Health Insurance Coverage, 7.*

22. U.S. Department of Health and Human Services, *Protecting Your Health Insurance Coverage, 6.*

23 U.S. Department of Health and Human Services, *Protecting Your Health Insurance Coverage, 24.*

24. See note 16 above.

25. Social Security Administration, *Social Security Handbook* (Baltimore: Social Security Administration, 2001), 111, 493–494.

26. Susan Milstrey Wells, *A Delicate Balance: Living Successfully with Chronic Illness* (New York and London: Insight Books, 1998), 203.

CHAPTER 5

1. Audrey Kron, *Meeting the Challenge*, 72. (This question originally appeared in *Meeting the Challenge* and was reproduced here with permission from Ms. Kron.)

2. For more information, go to http://capwiz.com/ama/home/.

3. Lee S. Berk, David L. Felten, Stanley A. Tan, Barry B. Bittman, and James Westengard, "Moducation of Neuroimmune Parameters During The Eustress of Humor-Associated Mirthful Laughter," *Alternative Therapies*, vol. 7, no. 2, (March 2001): 62–63.

4. P.M. Eng, E.B. Rimm, G. Fitzmaurice, I. Kawachi, "Social Ties and Change in Social Ties in Relation to Subsequent Total and Cause-specific Mortality and Coronary Heart Disease Incidence in Men," *American Journal of Epidemiology*, vol. 155, no. 8 (2002): 700–709. This ten year study of 28,369 American professional men between the ages of 42–77 showed that the men who were not as social were more likely to die than their more connected counterparts. "Deaths from accidents and suicide and from other noncancer, noncardiovascular causes were significantly increased among less socially connected men," the researchers concluded, adding that socially isolated men also had an increased risk of fatal coronary heart disease.

   Another relevant study is L.F. Berkman and S.L. Syme, "Social networks, host resistance, and mortality: a nine-year follow-up study of Alameda County residents," *American Journal of Epidemiology*, vol. 109, no. 2 (1979): 186–204. This nine-year study investigated several thousand adults in Alameda County, California and found that the more socially linked subjects were less likely to have died during the course of the study.

   A third is Ted Kaptchuk and Michael Croucher, *The Healing Arts: A Journey Through the Faces of Medicine* (London: British Broadcasting Corporation, 1986), 32. A government task force in Massachusetts looking into the determining factors for surviving atherosclerotic heart disease reported that the most reliable indicator was not related to smoking, blood pressure or cholesterol levels; it was "job satisfaction." The second best indicator: "overall happiness."

5. TransCanada Pipelines Rally For Muscular Dystrophy, "Danielle Campo," TransCanada Pipelines Rally For Muscular Dystrophy Web site, Internet, December 25, 2001. Available: http://www.transcanadarally.ca/english/danielle_bio.htm.

CHAPTER 6

1. Gregg Piburn, Beyond Chaos: *One Man's Journey Alongside His Chronically Ill Wife* (Atlanta: Arthritis Foundation, May, 1999), 230–233.

2. For more information on Pauline Salvucci's practice, go to www.selfcareconnection.com.

3. Diane Clehane, "Dana Reeve: Finding Strength in Letters," *The Westchester Wag,* December 1999, cover story.

CHAPTER 7

1. Camilla Cohee, "Making the Most of It," *Santa Barbara News-Press,* January 15, 2002, sec. A1.

2. Marvin Bartlett, *The Joy Cart: The True Story of a Boy and His Toys* (Baltimore: PublishAmerica, Inc., 2002).

CHAPTER 8

1. S. Laurance Johnston, "Prayer and Healing," Paraplegia News, vol. 53, no. 3 (March 1999): 23–25. The 94 percent figure was taken from a 1994 Gallup Poll.

2. William S. Harris, Manohar Gowda, Jerry W. Kolb, et al., "A Randomized, Controlled Trial of the Effects of Remote, Intercessory Prayer on Outcomes in Patients Admitted to the Coronary Care Unit," *Archives of Internal Medicine,* vol. 159, no. 19 (October 25, 1999): 2273–2278.

3. Fred Rosner, "Therapeutic Efficacy of Prayer," *Archives of Internal Medicine,* vol. 160, no. 12 (June 26, 2000): 1875.

4. Henry J. McQuay, R. Andrew Moore, Christopher Eccleston, Stephen Morely, Amanda C de C Williams, "Systematic Review of Outpatient Services for Chronic Pain Control," *Health Technology Assessment,* vol. 1, no. 6 (July 1997): 51.

5. National Institutes of Health, "Integration of Behavioral and Relaxation Approaches into the Treatment of Chronic Pain and Insomnia," National Institutes of Health, Technology Assessment Conference Statement No. 17, October 16–18, 1995, 1–34.

6. Carol Krucoff, Mitchell Krucoff, and Adam Brill, Healing Moves: How To Cure, Relieve, And Prevent Common Ailments With Exercise (New York: Harmony Books, 2000).

7. Norman Cousins, *Anatomy of an Illness as Perceived by the Patient* (New York: Bantam Dell Publishing Group, 1991), 29–39.

8. Stephanie E. Clipper, *Pain: Hope through Research* (Bethesda, MD: National Institute of Neurological Disorders and Stroke, National Institutes of Health, 2001), 23.

9. Gerald M. Aronoff, "Opioids in Chronic Pain Management: Is There a Significant Risk of Addiction?" *Current Pain and Headache Reports*, vol. 4, no. 2 (April 2000):112–121.

    Also S. R. Savage, "Opioid Therapy of Chronic Pain: Assessment of Consequences," *Acta Anaesthesiologica Scandinavica*, vol. 43, no. 9 (October 1999): 909–917.

    Also Jane E. Brody, "Misunderstood Opioids and Needless Pain," *New York Times*, January 22, 2002, personal health section.

    Also Jennifer P. Schneider, "Management of chronic non-cancer pain: a guide to appropriate use of opioids," *Journal of Care Management*, vol. 4, no. 4 (August 1998): 10–20.

RESOURCE GUIDE

LEGAL AND FINANCIAL AID
For People with Chronic Illnesses

Turn to these groups for help in researching your legal rights and to discover what your financial options are if you are unable to work.

Centers for Medicare and Medicaid Services
John F. Kennedy Federal Building
Room 2325
Boston, MA 02203-0003
617-565-1232
http://cms.hhs.gov

This federal agency operates the nation's Medicare and Medicaid programs and falls under the umbrella of the U.S. Department of Health and Human Services. Medicare is a low-cost, and in some cases, free, health insurance program for people sixty-five years or older. It is also available to some people under sixty-five who have disabilities. Medicaid is a joint federal and state insurance program for low-income individuals.

Disability and Business Technical Assistance Centers
800-949-4232
www.adata.org

The Technical Assistance program operates centers across the nation. These were developed to educate and train people on the Americans with Disabilities Act (ADA), the federal law that prohibits employers from discriminating against people with disabilities.

National Association of Protection and Advocacy Systems
900 Second Street, NE, Suite 211
Washington, D.C. 20002
202-408-9514
www.protectionandadvocacy.com

This organization operates federally mandated disability rights agencies across the country. You can look in the government pages in your phone book to locate the one nearest you, or call the program's national phone number listed above. P and A agencies provide legal representation and other advocacy services to people with disabilities. In addition to monitoring conditions at care centers, P and As make sure individuals with disabilities get full access to educational programs, financial entitlements, healthcare, accessible housing, and employment opportunities.

Patient Advocate Foundation
753 Thimble Shoals Boulevard, Suite B
Newport News, Virginia 23606
800-532-5774
www.patientadvocate.org

This nonprofit group puts out the *National Financial Resource Guidebook for Patients*, which breaks down the options available to patients who need financial relief for housing, food, transportation, childcare, and insurance deductibles. The resources are listed on a state-by-state basis, which makes it easy to track down help in your specific region. The foundation will send you your state's listings at no charge, or you can purchase the entire book.

U.S. Department of Justice, Disability Rights Division
950 Pennsylvania Avenue, NW
Washington, D.C. 20530
800-514-0301
www.usdoj.gov/crt/ada/adahom1.htm

The Department of Justice provides specialists who offer assistance and answer questions from employers and employees regarding the ADA.

U.S. Equal Employment Opportunity Commission
1801 L. Street, NW
Washington, D.C. 20507
800-669-4000
www.eeoc.gov

This agency enforces several national equal-rights laws, including the ADA. The organization is available to answer questions and assist in enforcement.

NATIONAL ORGANIZATIONS
Support Groups, Etc., by Illness

National nonprofits are a great place to start if you are researching your disease or are looking to contact other people with your illness. Call to find local chapters.

Alzheimer's
Alzheimer's Association
900 Second Street, NE, Suite 211
Washington, D.C. 20002
800-272-3900
www.alz.org

Alcoholism and Substance Abuse
Al-Anon Family Group Headquarters
1600 Corporate Landing Parkway
Virginia Beach, VA 23454-5617
757-563-1600
www.al-anon.org

Alcoholism and Substance Abuse (cont.)

Alcoholics Anonymous
475 Riverside Drive, 11th Floor
New York, NY 10115
www.alcoholics-anonymous.org

National Center on Addiction and Substance Abuse at Columbia University
633 Third Avenue, 19th Floor
New York, NY 10017-6706
212-841-5200
www.casacolumbia.org

National Institute on Alcohol Abuse and Alcoholism
6000 Executive Boulevard
Bethesda, MD 20892-7003
301-443-0595
www.niaaa.nih.gov

Arthritis

American College of Rheumatology
1800 Century Place, Suite 250
Atlanta, GA 30345
404-633-3777
www.rheumatology.org

Arthritis Foundation
1330 West Peachtree Street
Atlanta, GA 30309
800-283-7800
www.arthritis.org

Asthma

Allies Against Asthma
National Program Office
University of Michigan, School of Public Health
109 South Observatory Street
Ann Arbor, MI 48109-2029
734-615-3312
www.asthma.umich.edu

Attention Deficit Disorder
Children and Adults with Attention Deficit Disorders
8181 Professional Place, Suite 201
Landover, MD 20785
800-233-4050
www.chadd.com

Cancer
AMC Cancer Research Center and Foundation
1600 Pierce Street
Denver, CO 80214
800-321-1557
www.amc.org

American Association for Cancer Research
Public Ledger Building, Suite 826
150 South Independence Mall, West
Philadelphia, PA 19106-3483
215-440-9300
www.aacr.org

American Cancer Society
P.O. Box 102454
Atlanta, GA 30368-2454
800-ACS-2345
www.cancer.org

Cerebral Palsy
United States Cerebral Palsy Athletic Association
25 West Independence Way
Kingston, RI 02881
401-792-7130
www.uscpaa.org

Chronic Fatigue Syndrome
CFIDS Association of America
P.O. Box 220398
Charlotte, NC 28222-0398
800-442-3437
www.cfids.org

Chronic Fatigue Syndrome (cont.)
National CFIDS Foundation
103 Aletha Road
Needham, MA 02492
718-449-3535
www.ncf-net.org

Chronic Pain
American Chronic Pain Association
P.O. Box 850
Rocklin, CA 95677
800-533-3231
www.theacpa.org

Cystic Fibrosis
Cystic Fibrosis Foundation
6931 Arlington Road
Bethesda, MD 20814
800-FIGHT-CF
www.cff.org

Diabetes
American Diabetes Association
1701 North Beauregard Street
Alexandria, VA 22311
800-342-2383
www.diabetes.org

Diabetes Institutes Foundation
855 W. Brambleton Avenue
Norfolk, VA 23510
866-DIF-CURE or 757-446-8420
www.dif.org

Eating Disorders
Center for Change
1790 North State Street
Orem, UT 84057
888-224-8250
www.centerforchange.com

Eating Disorders (cont.)

Overeaters Anonymous
World Service Office
P.O. Box 44020
Rio Rancho, NM 87174-4020
505-891-2664
www.overeatersanonymous.org

Emphysema

American Lung Association
1740 Broadway
New York, NY 10019
212-315-8700
www.lungusa.org

Emphysema Foundation for Our Right to Survive
Claycomo Plaza
411 North East, U.S. Highway 69
Claycomo, MO 64119
816-452-3132
www.emphysema.net

Epilepsy

Epilepsy Foundation
4351 Garden City Drive
Landover, MD 20785-7223
800-332-1000
www.efa.org

Heart Disease

American Heart Association
7272 Greenville Avenue
Dallas, TX 75231
800-242-9721
www.americanheart.org

Hemophilia

National Hemophilia Foundation
116 W. 32nd Street, 11th Floor
New York, NY 10001
800-424-2634
www.hemophilia.org

Hepatitis
HealthTalk
Hepatitis C Education Network
201 Queen Anne Avenue North, Suite 400
Seattle, WA 98109
206-352-4066
www.healthtalk.com

Hepatitis Foundation International
30 Sunrise Terrace
Cedar Grove, NJ 07009-1423
800-891-0707
www.hepfi.org

Hepatitis Information Network
3535 Trans-Canada Highway
Pointe Claire, Quebec H9R 1B4
www.hepnet.com

HIV/AIDS
HIV/AIDS Treatment and Information Service
P.O. Box 6303
Rockville, MD 20849-6303
800-HIV-0440
www.hivatis.org

National Association of People with AIDS
1413 K Street, NW
Washington, DC 20005
202-898-0414
www.napwa.org

Gastrointestinal Disorders
Crohn's and Colitis Foundation of America
386 Park Avenue South, 17th Floor
New York, NY 10016-8804
800-932-2423
www.ccfa.org

Hypertension
American Society of Hypertension
515 Madison Avenue, Suite 1212
New York, NY 10022
212-644-0650
www.ash-us.org

Kidney Disease

American Association of Kidney Patients
3505 East Frontage Road, Suite 315
Tampa, FL 33607
800-749-2257
www.aakp.org

American Kidney Fund
6110 Executive Boulevard, Suite 1010
Rockville, MD 20852
800-638-8299
www.akfinc.org

iKidney (sponsored by Watson Pharmaceuticals)
311 Bonnie Circle
Corona, CA 92878
800-249-5499
www.iKidney.com

Life Options Rehabilitation Resource Center
c/o Medical Education Institute
414 D'Onofrio Drive, Suite 200
Madison, WI 53719
800-468-7777
www.lifeoptions.org

National Kidney Foundation
30 East 33rd Street, Suite 1100
New York, NY 10016
800-622-9010
www.kidney.org

Liver Disease

American Association for the Study of Liver Diseases
1729 King Street, Suite 200
Alexandria, VA 22314
703-299-9766
www.aasld.org

American Liver Foundation
75 Maiden Lane, Suite 603
New York, NY 10038
800-GOLIVER
www.liverfoundation.org

Lung Disease
American Lung Association
1740 Broadway
New York, NY 10019
212-315-8700
www.lungusa.org

Lupus
Lupus Foundation of America
1300 Piccard Drive, Suite 200
Rockville, MD 20850-4303
301-670-9292
www.lupus.org

Mental Illness
Center for Addiction and Mental Health Foundation
33 Russell Street, 2nd Floor
Toronto, Ontario M5S 2S1
800-414-0471
www.camh.net

National Alliance for the Mentally Ill
Colonial Place Three
2107 Wilson Boulevard, Suite 300
Arlington, VA 22201
800-950-NAMI
www.nami.org

Migraine
M.A.G.N.U.M.
Migraine Awareness Group
113 South Saint Asaph, Suite 300
Alexandria, VA 22314
703-739-9384
www.migraines.org

Multiple Sclerosis
Multiple Sclerosis Education Network (Health Talk Interactive)
201 Queen Anne Avenue North, Suite 400
Seattle, WA 98109
206-352-4066
www.healthtalk.com

Multiple Sclerosis (cont.)

Multiple Sclerosis Foundation
6350 North Andrews Avenue
Fort Lauderdale, FL 33309-2130
800-225-6495
www.msfacts.org

UCSF Multiple Sclerosis Center
350 Parnassus Avenue, Suite 908
San Francisco, CA 94117
415-514-1684
http://mscenter.his.ucsf.edu

Muscular Dystrophy

Muscular Dystrophy Association
3300 East Sunrise Drive
Tucson, AZ 85718
800-572-1717
www.mdausa.org

Muscular Dystrophy Family Foundation
2330 North Meridian Street
Indianapolis, IN 46208-5730
800-544-1213
www.mdff.org

Osteoporosis

Foundation for Osteoporosis Research and Education
300 27th Street
Oakland, CA 94612
888-266-3015
www.fore.org

National Osteoporosis Foundation
1232 22nd Street, NW
Washington, DC 20037-1292
202-223-2226
www.nof.org

Parkinson's Disease

American Parkinson's Disease Association
1250 Hylan Boulevard, Suite 4B
Staten Island, NY 10305-1946
800-223-2732
www.apdaparkinson.com

Parkinson's Disease (cont.)
Parkinson's Disease Foundation
710 West 168th Street
New York, NY 10032-9982
800-457-6676
www.pdf.org

Scleroderma
Scleroderma Foundation
12 Kent Way, Suite 101
Byfield, MA 01922
800-722-4673
www.scleroderma.org

Sickle Cell Disease
Sickle Cell Disease Association of America
200 Corporate Point, Suite 495
Culver City, CA 90230-8727
800-421-8453
www.sicklecelldisease.org

Spina Bifida
Spina Bifida Association of America
4590 MacArthur Boulevard, NW, Suite 250
Washington, DC 20007-4226
800-621-3141
www.sbaa.org

Spinal Cord
Christopher Reeve Paralysis Foundation
500 Morris Avenue
Springfield, NJ 07801
800-225-0292
www.apacure.com

Foundation for Spinal Cord Injury Prevention and Cure
19223 Roscommon
Harper Woods, MI 48225
800-342-0330
www.fscip.org

Spinal Cord (cont.)
Kent Waldrep National Paralysis Foundation
16415 Addison Road, Suite 550
Addison, TX 75001
877-724-2873
www.spinalvictory.org

Stroke
National Institute of Neurological Disorders and Stroke
National Institutes of Health
P.O. Box 5801
Bethesda, MD 20824
800-352-9424
www.ninds.nih.gov

National Stroke Association
9707 East Easter Lane
Englewood, CO 80112
800-STROKES
www.stroke.org

INDEX

241

Chronically Happy

Joyful Living in Spite of Chronic Illness
By Lori Hartwell

For more information or to order *Chronically Happy* visit www.chronicallyhappy.com or contact the publisher at:

POETIC MEDIA PRESS
505 Beach Street, Penthouse
San Francisco, California 94133
Telephone orders: 415-447-4800 Ext.4
Email orders: orders@chronicallyhappy.com

We accept major credit cards, money orders and checks. Make check payable to: Poetic Media, Inc.

Price

$12.95 U.S.
$14.95 Canada
(Plus shipping and handling)

Shipping and Handling Options

1. USPS Book Rate $3.50 (approximately eight day delivery)
2. USPS Priority Mail $5.50 (two-three day delivery)
(California residents add sales tax)

To Contact the Author

E-mail: lori@chronicallyhappy.com
Write to:
Lori Hartwell
1102 N. Brand Blvd. #74
Glendale, California 91202

Check out the *Chronically Happy* Web site at www.chronicallyhappy.com for Lori's scheduled book signings, speaking engagements, and additional information.

Chronically Happy

Joyful Living in Spite of Chronic Illness
By Lori Hartwell

For more information or to order *Chronically Happy* visit www.chronicallyhappy.com or contact the publisher at:

POETIC MEDIA PRESS
505 Beach Street, Penthouse
San Francisco, California 94133
Telephone orders: 415-447-4800 Ext.4
Email orders: orders@chronicallyhappy.com

We accept major credit cards, money orders and checks. Make check payable to: Poetic Media, Inc.

Price
$12.95 U.S.
$14.95 Canada
(Plus shipping and handling)

Shipping and Handling Options
1. USPS Book Rate $3.50 (approximately eight day delivery)
2. USPS Priority Mail $5.50 (two-three day delivery)
(California residents add sales tax)

To Contact the Author
E-mail: lori@chronicallyhappy.com
Write to:
Lori Hartwell
1102 N. Brand Blvd. #74
Glendale, California 91202

Check out the *Chronically Happy* Web site at www.chronicallyhappy.com for Lori's scheduled book signings, speaking engagements, and additional information.